# I'M A CHRISTIAN SO HOW CAN I HAVE DEMONS?

A GUIDE TO DEMONS AND DELIVERANCE

*BY JOSEPH THOMPSON*

**I'm a Christian so how can I have demons?**



Edited by Patton Dodd

Cover design by Tim Jaycox

Printed by: Litho Press, Inc.
4334 Milling Road
San Antonio, TX



To order additional copies of this book or other resources by the author, write to Yeshua Ministries, P.O. Box 62325, Colorado Springs, CO 80962, or call 719.598.9489, or email: jt2yeshua@cs.com.

ISBN 0-9719-5348-1
Printed in the United States of America
1. Spiritual Warfare. I. Title

# Table Of Contents

***To my precious wife Sola and to my indefatigable kids Demi, Bimi and Temi.***

***The journey is worthwhile because of you.***

# *Acknowledgements*

I have looked forward to the day when I would write the acknowledgements for this book. It has been a long time in the making and I have often wondered what I would say when the time came. You see I am one of those people who really enjoy reading the author's acknowledgements. I imagine it's because, in addition to the well-deserved pats on the back, they give me insight into the heart and the experiences of the writer.

This book is truly a reflection of my heart. I burn with the passion that longs to see whole cities and nations transformed through a clearer understanding of deliverance and spiritual warfare in the Church. I began this book in its original form about nine years ago (it has turned out to be a completely different work from the original manuscript) and this is the result of long, arduous hours of research, practical hands-on experience and continued revelation by the Holy Spirit. It is fitting therefore that thanks and gratitude go to my heavenly Father.

Thank you, Tunde Ogunnaike, for all of the time and effort you invested in our relationship and in discipling me all those years ago. Thanks, Anselm and Connie. Without you guys I wouldn't even have begun to understand deliverance. My gratitude goes to Patton Dodd for all the tireless hours you invested editing the manuscript and challenging me to become a better writer. To my dearest friends, Mike Fehlauer and Jeff Tarbox, you have continually inspired me to become all that God wants me to be. To Ted Haggard and Steve Brooks, quintessential Pastors. To my ministry team: Karen, Kaye and Lisa (whom Pastor Gilbert calls The Three Musketeers), Gary and Kathy, Scott and Kim, Megan and my faithful disciples Keith and Eava, thanks for all the memories. We have only just begun the journey. No doubt we will have lots more "underwear" stories (sorry folks, an inside joke!) to tell over the years.

I want to thank my wife Sola, my best friend and my biggest fan. All your suggestions and pre-edits have made this book better than anything I could have written on my own. Thanks for "being there" and knowing when I needed a wife, a friend or just a listening ear. Last but not least, I want to thank my wonderful kids, Demi, Bimi and Temi for recognizing that the call to ministry is not just Dad's call but our family's call. You guys are special and I love you deeply.

Joseph Thompson

Colorado Springs

March 2002

# Can a Christian have demons?

For years, she knelt at the altar every Sunday—broken, contrite, and weeping uncontrollably. For years, her life was a blurry nightmare, a painful and unending tromp from one strange bed to another.

None of them mattered anymore…not that they ever did. She hoped in vain that maybe, just maybe, one of them would turn out to be that perfect relationship that would finally help pull her out of the mire of shame and depression. She wore a cloak of darkness and lived a life of second chances. But the perfect relationship never came, and so she continued to come to the altar to weep and pray.

Two years ago, she became a Christian. She was told that her newfound faith would bring an end to her self-destructive slide. She believed her church friends when they told her that once she became a Christian she would be totally free from all of those destructive desires. But her habits never changed, and she was in more pain now than ever before.

What was the problem? Could it be that she wasn't really a Christian after all? Maybe if she responded to the altar call often enough, God would see that she was sincere and rid her of this destructive pattern.

And was it really her fault that she couldn't stay faithful to one man? If only her parents had shown more of an interest in her instead of devoting all their time to building a business, maybe none of this would have happened.

But every day, memories of her uncle in a drunken stupor continually violating her twelve-year-old body brought images of terror and left her feeling used and dirty. Years of counseling and therapy hadn't helped, though her parents seemed to derive a sense of exoneration from their guilt through these sessions. But they weren't the ones who had to live with the memories. They didn't know what it was like to awaken in terror every time you heard a floorboard creak. It had gone on for four years under their own roof, and they never even suspected.

Now, twenty years later, she had lost track of how many men there had been, and how many sexual addiction therapy sessions she attended. All she wanted was to rid herself of the pain and guilt. And she had nowhere to turn. So she kept returning to the altar each Sunday, hoping against hope that something would give, and light would break through…

Sadly, churches are replete with people like this—people who don't know where to turn for help. Somehow, they've gotten the unbiblical idea that being a Christian means that their lives should be problem-free, that they will never struggle with sin and addictions. When their problems continue, they just try to cover them up or forget them. Many hide behind sex, drugs or some other outlet that provides a temporary respite from the harsh realities of everyday living. And even when they decide to "give it to God" at the altar, they almost immediately pick up right where they left off before they came to the altar.

How convenient for our adversary the devil. A Christian who is weakened by sin and who struggles with guilt and shame from their past is certainly less threatening to Satan's rule and authority than a Christian living victoriously. Little wonder, then, that deliverance is one aspect of ministry in the Church that he would like to keep silently covered up.

Sorry Old-Slew-Foot, this time your scheme has failed.

For fifteen years, I have counseled Christians through the process of deliverance. All of the people I minister to live apparently normal

Christian lives, and many are pastors or leaders in ministry. But they all have some secret problem, some hidden pain that haunts them daily and keeps them from experiencing the fullness of life in Christ. Some suspect that their problems may be demonic, but many don't believe that Christians can be affected by demons.

This is a common conception in the Body of Christ. Some denominations have elaborate theologies to attest to this belief, and many Christians don't think their problems can be linked to anything demonic simply because they are Christians.

"The Bible says that he whom the Son sets free is free indeed, right?" they say. "How could a demon occupy the same place in my spirit that God occupies? I thought light and dark couldn't inhabit the same place."

Good questions. It's certainly understandable that we don't want to believe that demons can influence us—it's a scary thought, and one that doesn't line up with a lot of what we've been taught about what "the Christian life" is supposed to be like.

But there is good evidence, both biblically and experientially, that demons can and do influence Christians.

## Veronica

She had no idea what to expect. Veronica had been invited to attend the deliverance class by a friend who told her that she might find answers to some of the questions that had continually plagued her. A well-raised, good Lutheran girl, Veronica had never encountered anything quite like this before.

I noticed her the moment she walked into the room. Maybe it was that her out-of-place feeling showed on her face. For whatever reason I made a mental note to observe her deliverance session. After the teaching portion of the class concluded, I began to assign people to groups so that everyone who needed ministry would have an opportunity to receive it. I assigned Veronica to a group that included my brother-in-law (a minister visiting from England) as one of the ministers, and after everyone had been assigned, the ministry began.

As is my habit, I began to go from group to group discerning a spirit here or giving a word of encouragement there. This went on for a while with people receiving their deliverance and rejoicing. Finally, I arrived at the group that Veronica was a part of and observed that my brother-in-law and a couple of the female ministers had taken her aside to pray for her separately from the rest of the group. I joined them and immediately began to discern a number of spirits that were in operation. The strongest sense I had was that there was a spirit of death on Veronica. I began to address this spirit along with other spirits I discerned until I sensed that there was freedom.

After the session I asked Veronica to fill me in on what she had been dealing with. She explained how she had been struggling with a debilitating medical condition for months that had puzzled the doctors and had left her feeling confused and unclear as to what God's purpose was in the midst of all this turmoil. I met with Veronica on a number of occasions subsequent to that, and am fully persuaded that the devil had assigned a spirit of death to take her life through sickness. On one of our subsequent meetings, Veronica told me how, as I had prayed for her and discerned a spirit of death, she immediately felt a stirring in her gut, almost as if someone had squeezed the air out of her lungs. By her own admission, she felt as if something had instantly left her.

Now, Veronica, because of her Lutheran background, was unable to articulate in "Charismatic-ese" exactly what had taken place. She is, however, aware enough of her body to be able to establish that she was delivered from a spirit of death that day.

How can this be? Where does the Bible teach that Christians can suffer from demonic influences?

## Searching for the truth

In the mid-to-late 1980s, I was living in Lagos, Nigeria. I had only recently become a Christian and was involved with a number of Christian groups, one of which was a college campus fellowship at the University of Lagos, where my sister and her husband (then her fiancé) were leaders.

One of the teachings that was strongly emphasized there was that Christians could not have demons because they were new creations in Christ and old things were passed away, all had become new (2 Corinthians 5:17). This teaching troubled me. I saw too many Christians struggling with addictions, various hereditary issues, as well as depression. If old things were passed away, why were all these carryovers from their pre-Christ life still an issue?

During that same period, I had some friends who were involved in the ministry of deliverance. I asked them if they ever ministered to Christians, and they assured me that their ministry was geared towards Christians. I was amazed by the fact that they were able to articulate the biblical basis for deliverance to Christians quite clearly from the Scriptures. They explained that 2 Corinthians 5:17 was a reference to our spiritual standing in Christ; the sins of our pre-Christ life were no longer a witness against us because we had been washed clean in the shed blood of Christ, but we could still be influenced by demons.

This was quite different from anything I had ever heard. Intrigued, I began to research it for myself. The rest of this chapter is the story of what I found....

## What the Bible really says about Christians and deliverance: A primer

### 1. Deliverance is *primarily* for believers

In Mark 7:24-30, we are told the story of a woman whose young daughter was demon-possessed:

> From there [Jesus] arose and went to the region of Tyre and Sidon. And He entered a house and wanted no one to know it, but He could not be hidden. For a woman whose young daughter had an unclean spirit heard about Him, and she came and fell at His feet. The woman was a Greek, a Syro-Phoenician by birth, and she kept asking Him to cast the demon out of her daughter. But Jesus said to her, "Let the children be filled first, for it is not good to take the children's bread and throw it to the little dogs." And she answered and

> said to Him, "Yes, Lord, yet even the little dogs under the table eat from the children's crumbs." Then He said to her, "For this saying go your way; the demon has gone out of your daughter." And when she had come to her house, she found the demon gone out, and her daughter lying on the bed.
> - Mark 7:24-30

This woman was not Jewish, but of foreign descent. The picture we are given is one of a person who did not have a covenant relationship with Jesus but wanted a touch of His power.

The centerpiece of this passage is Jesus' startling statement: "Let the *children* be *filled* first, for it is not good to take the children's *bread* and throw it to the little *dogs*." Let's examine definitions of the italicized words, and then re-read Jesus' statement with those definitions in mind.

**Children:** There are 14 different translations of the word "children" in the original Greek, but the one used here is *teknon*[1], meaning a child that is produced, a son or daughter. It is from a root word *timē*[2] (ti-may), meaning valuable, precious or something of high price.

**Filled:** This is the Greek word *chörtazó*[3] (khor-tad-zo) which means to supply in abundance, to feed, fill or satisfy.

**Bread:** "Bread" is the Greek word *artos*[4], which means raised or leavened bread. Its root word is the word *airo*[5] which, by implication, means to expiate (do away with) sin; loose, remove, take away from. [Here, bread is a metaphor for what the woman wants from Jesus: freedom for her daughter.]

**Dogs:** The Greek word is *kunariön*[6], which is itself a derivative of the word *kuön*[7], which both literally and figuratively means a dog or a puppy ("hound").

Now let's re-read the verse with the above definitions inserted:

> But Jesus said to her, "Let those that are sons and daughters by reason of the high price I have paid be supplied abundantly to satisfaction first, for it is not good to take the cleansing and freedom intended for my valuable sons and daughters and throw it to the dogs."

In other words, Jesus is telling the woman that deliverance—the very thing she was asking for—is primarily reserved for people who are in covenant relationship with Him. Not only is deliverance for believers, but it is *primarily* for believers!

(Aside: His emphasis on taking what belongs to the children and giving it to the dogs is in no way comparing the value of a non-Christian to that of a dog. He is merely illustrating the stark contrast between the Christian and the non-Christian. In one sense it can be seen as comparing the worth a dog would place on something that was extremely valuable to a human. One that is not in covenant relationship with Jesus places very little value on the price that was paid for salvation and all its attendant blessings, including deliverance.)

## 2. Deliverance is not intended for non-believers.

In Luke 11:24-26 the Bible says:

> When an unclean spirit goes out of a man, he goes through dry places, seeking rest; and finding none, he says, 'I will return to my house from which I came.' And when he comes, he finds it swept and put in order. Then he goes and takes with him seven other spirits more wicked than himself, and they enter and dwell there; and the last state of that man is worse than the first."

Evidently the demons that are cast out seek to return to their house or host. The only way they are able to re-enter is if the host is "swept," that is, devoid of the word of God, and "put in order," or garnished, which means to be adorned with the world.

Now, by this understanding, a non-Christian is both swept and put in order - they don't have the word of God in them, and they are adorned with the world. So, we do the non-Christian a disservice by ministering deliverance to him when he is not firmly grounded in the knowledge of the truth. The only evidence in Scripture of Jesus doing deliverance on one who did not believe in Him was the demoniac of Gadara (Luke 8:26-33). I believe that Jesus did deliverance on him because the demons stood as a hindrance to his ability to recognize and receive the lordship of Christ. This argument seems strengthened by the fact that after he was delivered, he acknowledged the lordship of Jesus and went throughout his entire city, "evangelizing."

### 3. Demons do not possess a Christian's spirit.

It should be noted that demons do not possess a person's spirit (except under extreme cases of Satanic ritual abuse, etc.), for they themselves are disembodied spirits. They only need a body to function through, so the argument as to whether or not Christians can be possessed is, in fact, a moot point. That is why the Bible tells us that Jesus cast the demons (or permitted them) into the herd of swine. Animals do not have spirits; only humans are made in the image and likeness of God. The demons do not need a spirit to work through - they need a body. Furthermore, the Bible teaches us in Mark 16:17 that in the name of Jesus, we shall cast out demons, not cast off demons. You cannot cast out what is not within.

### Types and shadows of deliverance

The Bible is replete with what we call "types and shadows" of deliverance that speak to how demons can and do influence the people of God. A "type" is a biblical picture from either the Old or New Testament that refers to specific people or events that are analogous of things to come—for example, Noah is a type of the Church in that he was saved out of the destruction of the world through the grace of God.

A "shadow" is a prophetic picture also from the Old or New Testaments, foretelling events in the future. For example, in Isaiah 53:5 there is a graphic foretelling of Jesus' sacrificial death, which would redeem the world from sin: "But he was wounded for our transgressions, He was bruised for our iniquities; the chastisement for our peace was upon Him, and by His stripes we are healed." If the claims and evidence to Jesus' death and resurrection are true, then this is clearly a reference to Him. Since Isaiah lived approximately 700 years before Christ, he had to have had divine insight into the fact that Jesus would be beaten (39 stripes), wounded and bruised in order for mankind's redemption to be fulfilled. This kind of prophetic insight revealing the picture of a future event is a shadow.

When I read the Bible, I am constantly looking for these types and shadows. These are clues that give us insight into the ways of God and what it means to be a Christian. The Bible is full of such clues, and they are especially useful when examining something like demons and deliverance.

## Exodus from Egypt—and demonic strongholds

The wonderful story of the liberation of the Israelites from Egypt is a shadow of deliverance. In this story, Moses is a type of Jesus, Pharaoh is a type of Satan, and the Israelites are a type of the Church. Exodus 5:1-9 says:

> Afterward Moses and Aaron went in and told Pharaoh, "Thus says the Lord God of Israel: 'Let My people go, that they may hold a feast to Me in the wilderness.'" And Pharaoh said, "Who is the Lord, that I should obey His voice to let Israel go? I do not know the Lord, nor will I let Israel go." So they said, "The God of the Hebrews has met with us. Please, let us go three days' journey into the desert and sacrifice to the Lord our God, lest He fall upon us with pestilence or with the sword." Then the king of Egypt said to them, "Moses and Aaron, why do you take the people from their work? Get back to your labor." And Pharaoh said, "Look, the people of the land are many now, and you make them rest from their labor!" So the same day Pharaoh commanded the taskmasters of the people and their officers, saying,
>
> "You shall no longer give the people straw to make brick as before. Let them go and gather straw for themselves. And you shall lay on them the quota of bricks which they made before. You shall not reduce it. For they are idle; therefore they cry out, saying, 'Let us go and sacrifice to our God.' Let more work be laid on the men, that they may labor in it, and let them not regard false words."

Pharaoh is a picture of Satan as a hard "taskmaster." Refusing to acknowledge the lordship of Jesus, he holds the people of God captive to sin and demonic influences. These hinder our ability to walk fully in the life of God (offering worship and the sacrifice of our lives) and cause us to reflect a tarnished image of the realities of kingdom living to a lost world.

Previously, the people of Israel had been welcome guests in Egypt and had enjoyed favor at the highest levels of power as a result of Joseph's influence while he was alive. According to Exodus 1:8, "After Joseph's death, there arose a new king over Egypt, who did not know Joseph." Suddenly the Israelites went from being favored guests to a threat to national security. This new Pharaoh came to a radical conclusion:

> And he said to his people, "Look, the people of the children of Israel are more and mightier than we; come, let us deal shrewdly with them, lest they multiply, and it happen, in the event of war, that they also join our enemies and fight against us, and go up out of the land." – Exodus 1:9-10

Pharaoh enslaves the Israelites and they become the cheapest source of labor in Egypt. The manifestations of Satan's demonic strongholds are not dissimilar. Having enslaved the world to sin, sickness and the demonic, he refuses to release them even though Christ (like Moses did to Pharaoh) has instructed him to do so. The Bible says God hardened Pharaoh's heart so that he would not release the Israelites. I believe that the reason for this was to enable God display His authority over the false gods (demonic strongholds) of Egypt.

This belief is strengthened by the fact that later on God speaks to Moses and says; "Now you shall see what I will do to Pharaoh. For with a strong hand (under heavy pressure) he will let them go, and with a strong hand he will drive them out of his land" (Exodus 6:1).

By the same token, demonic forces do not willingly relinquish their stronghold on a person's life. It is interesting to note that each of the ten plagues that came upon Egypt were confronting specific gods (demonic strongholds), effectively rendering those strongholds impotent. In other words, since the Egyptians worshipped a multiplicity of gods, they had gods over everything. They had gods over the Nile, over cattle, grain, death and life, among numerous other gods. The plagues that were directed against each one of these areas were a direct affront to these gods. They demonstrated the power of Moses' God as being far superior to that of the Egyptian gods. The final blow was struck against the sun god, Amun Ra. Considered the supreme deity in Egypt, he was represented by Pharaoh on earth. Ra's authority was rendered impotent by the plagues of darkness and death of the first born son in every Egyptian household including Pharaohs. In the same way, deliverance is a confrontation of spiritual strongholds with the light of the Word of God that renders Satan's stronghold over our lives impotent.

## Raising Lazarus, liberating believers

In the New Testament, the miraculous resurrection of Lazarus is a perfect shadow of both salvation and deliverance in believers' lives. Lazarus and his sisters Mary and Martha are particularly good friends of Jesus'. He has dined at their home on numerous occasions (John 11:2; 12:1-3) and certainly they have shared a few good laughs together.

Suddenly, their world seems to crumble before their very eyes. Lazarus becomes deathly ill and, recognizing the healing powers possessed by Jesus, Mary and Martha request His immediate presence.

Jesus, however, has other plans. In John 11:6, we read "when He heard that (Lazarus) was sick, He stayed two more days in the place where He was." Amazingly, Jesus chooses to stay away two more days after hearing of Lazarus' illness. In the meantime, Lazarus dies.

According to verse 17, by the time Jesus arrives in Bethany (presumably a two-day journey from where He was), Lazarus has been in the tomb for four days. Mary and Martha are not only grief-stricken, but also puzzled by Jesus' apparent lack of sensitivity to their brother's plight.

However, Jesus has a plan. Jewish tradition held that when a person died, their soul would hover around the body for three days before departing. Jesus probably wanted to dispel any notion that Lazarus might still have been alive. When Jesus asks for the stone sealing the tomb to be removed, Martha states, "Lord, by this time there is a stench, for he has been dead four days." There is no doubt about it—Lazarus was dead!

Lazarus is a type of the believer. Dead in our sin, we are separated from God and carry with us the "stench" of the world that continually alienates us from God. We are sealed in the grave of despair and hopelessness until Jesus arrives with the keys of life and victory.

In John 11:41, Jesus stands at the opening to the tomb of Lazarus and prays to the Father. Then He shouts, "Lazarus come forth!" Jesus calls Lazarus from death to life—just as He calls believers from spiritual death to eternal life.

Lazarus was now "born again" and restored to life in Christ and by Christ. But he was bound with the "tokens of death" symbolized by the grave clothes on his hands and feet, and the cloth wrapped around his face (v. 44). Jesus turns to those around Him and asks them to "loose him, and let him go."

In other words, Jesus tells them to help Lazarus until he is able to walk on his own. Lazarus cannot be completely stable until his hands and feet are mobilized, and his eyes are free to see. Likewise, believers cannot completely reflect the nature and character of God until they are freed from the judgments and condemnations of the demonic strongholds of life before Christ. These are all symbolized by the grave-clothes on Lazarus' hands and feet and the cloth wrapped around his face, limiting his ability to see, smell, hear, feel or walk. Collectively, these are the "tokens of death" that hinder Lazarus' ability to live a full and effective life despite the fact that he has been raised from the dead.

As in the case of Lazarus, it is not until fellow believers in Jesus have helped to loose the grave-clothes from around those who have just experienced salvation, that we will see them experience the fullness of what Jesus has provided for them by raising them up from death to life.

The reality of the Christian experience suggests the need for a "spiritual-house-cleaning" after salvation or "rebirth." If Lazarus represents a true type of the Christian, then it is possible to be a Christian and still struggle with demonic influences.

Heavy theological debate continues to rage on about whether or not Christians can have demons. In the meantime, people will continue to struggle and search for ways to be set free. As the debate rages on, the truth silently speaks for itself.

# Sacred Cows

When it comes to deliverance, people have what I like to call "sacred cows." Sacred cows are things that people are not willing to give up. In deliverance, these sacred cows are notions or opinions about deliverance that aren't helpful to ministry. Some say all Christians are somehow possessed, some say Christians can only be influenced or oppressed. Some say people must physically manifest demons in order for there to be genuine healing, others claim that manifestations should never be allowed. Extreme positions run amuck, and, as with most areas of life, it's important to strike a balance and discover a healthy perspective on all these issues.

In this chapter, we'll look at a few of the most popular sacred cows: Should manifestation be allowed? Does deliverance solve the problem once and for all? Should there be a specific ministry of deliverance? When someone has problems with demons, are they always possessed, or just influenced? And what do we do with all those deliverance "weirdoes"?!

**To manifest or not to manifest, that is the question**

Jesus did deliverance often enough, and sometimes there were manifestations, sometimes not. Manifestations certainly cannot serve as the all-inclusive evidence of a successful deliverance. At the same time, I do not think that manifestations should be discounted in any way. Below is a partial list of some demonic manifestations along with biblical references:

Speaking

Convulsions

Violence

Spitting

Gnashing of teeth

Attempting to destroy their victim

Screaming (shouting)

Weakness after deliverance (being rigid and physically weakened)

> Now there was a man in their synagogue with an unclean spirit. ***And he cried out, saying, "Let us alone***! What have we to do with you, Jesus of Nazareth? Did you come to destroy us? I know who you are - the holy one of God!" But Jesus rebuked him, saying, "be quiet, and come out of him!" And ***when the unclean spirit had convulsed him*** and ***cried out with a loud voice, he came out of him***. Then they were all amazed, so that they questioned among themselves, saying, "what is this? What new doctrine is this? For with authority he commands even the unclean spirits, and they obey him." And immediately his fame spread throughout all the region around Galilee.

> Then one of the crowd answered and said, "Teacher, I brought you my son, who has a mute spirit. ***And wherever it seizes him***, ***it throws him down***, ***he foams at the mouth***, ***gnashes his teeth, and becomes rigid***... ***and often he has thrown him both into the fire and into the water to destroy him***... ***Then the spirit cried out***, ***convulsed him greatly***, and came out of him. ***And he became as one dead***, so that many said, "he is dead." But Jesus took him by the hand and lifted him up, and he arose.

-Mark 9: 17, 18, 22, 26, 27

## Angel's demons

In the last chapter, I mentioned that while living in Lagos, Nigeria, I met a group of Christians who had a deliverance ministry geared toward other believers. At one point, they invited me to attend one of their sessions as an observer.

I recall being amazed at the number and diversity of Christians that came to attend the deliverance session. The ministry began quite normally with the pastor teaching through Scriptures on deliverance. People were riveted to their seats in rapt attention. After the teaching, he asked the crowd to stand to their feet and move the chairs against the walls so that there would be room for everyone to stand in the center of the room. Then he began to pray and call out the names of certain demonic spirits. Immediately, some of the people in the room began to contort and gyrate and let out piercing screams.

The pastor and his ministry team began to minister to individual people. Watching closely, I observed that as he would discern a spirit and address it by name, the individual's facial expressions would contort with fear or anger or pain. He would command the spirit to leave; sometimes, it seemed that they would leave almost instantaneously with a piercing scream, while at other times there would be a look of defiance on the person's face. The more he addressed the spirit, the more defiant the person's expression became. Finally, he would ask the spirit to identify its point of entry and why it would not leave. To my surprise, the spirit would speak out of the person in a deep, guttural voice (whether the person was male or female). Usually, it would say it had entered at a traumatic point in the person's life or through some ancestral or generational curse.

One of the more dramatic deliverances I participated in was with a young lady (we will call her Angel) who had been involved with the occult and had recently become sexually involved with a young man. Apparently, after their exploits one night, Angel and her boyfriend had both experienced a tremendous sense of heaviness and had been unable to sleep all night. By their own admission, they had been embroiled in a heavy spiritual battle the entire night and were physically, emotionally and spiritually exhausted.

The next morning was a Sunday. We were preparing for the early morning service and I happened to be standing outside the main entrance of the church when I saw them both walking toward me. They looked as if they had been physically assaulted. As soon as they caught my eye, Angel stopped dead in her tracks, staring at me with a glazed look in her eyes and terror written across her face.

As I began to walk towards them, wondering if I had done something to offend her, she quickly walked across the street to the opposite side, all the while focusing on me with the terrified look. I reached the young man and he fell into my arms and broke down, sobbing.

He began to explain the events of the previous night. I walked with him over to the head of our deliverance team, to whom the young man recounted the events he had just explained to me. We agreed that we would wait until the conclusion of the second service (about 1:00 p.m.), and then pray for their deliverance. I was assigned to stay with them until then.

We walked back to where Angel was standing. As I approached, she began to back away, trembling. It suddenly dawned on me that there was a spiritual battle for control going on inside of her—every time I approached, the demons clearly went into fits, recognizing they were around spiritual power that was far greater than theirs.

I rebuked the demons in the name of Jesus and told them that I did not give them permission to manifest themselves. I spoke gently to Angel and explained what we had agreed on for deliverance. We decided in the meantime to wait inside a small diner that was across the street from the church.

We entered the diner and sat down at a table. All the while, the conflict inside Angel raged. She went from shaking uncontrollably with her eyes glazed over to laughing hysterically, her expression switching from defiance to anger, then to fear.

At this point, one of the most bizarre events began to unfold before my eyes. Into the diner walked a black hen (suffice it to say that I had never before seen an all-black hen, not to mention one walking into a diner). Angel's gaze fixed upon the hen as it casually walked over to a vacant chair about ten feet away from us. Without flinching or removing her gaze from the hen, I heard Angel say, in a measured, even tone, "I want an egg!"

I got up from where I was sitting and strode over to where the hen was perched upon the chair. As I got within a few feet of it, it jumped off the chair and took off for the exit. There, sitting where the hen had been, lay the largest egg I had ever seen. I picked it up and brought it back to the table. The terror on Angel's face was, as it appeared, about to send her into an apoplectic fit. As I held the egg out to her, she cowered in fear and hid her eyes behind her hands.

I began to prod her for information. She explained how she had been a "Bride of Satan" and how she had this beautiful mansion underwater by one of the well-known beaches in the city. She further explained that in the egg were the ten children she had had through "spiritual" sexual intercourse with Satan. My head spun as I tried to assimilate all this information and its implication for the impending deliverance.

I held onto the egg until the end of the second service, when I met with the entire deliverance team and briefed them on the bizarre events of the morning. We proceeded to the deliverance room where we started to minister to Angel. There were six of us, and we began the process as we would any other deliverance session, finding out from Angel what she had been involved in and what her background was. Some of the things we found out sounded like stories from an occult fiction novel, while others don't even bear repeating on paper.

Angel had been involved in witchcraft, and came from a broken home where her mother had also been involved in witchcraft. She explained that she had become involved in perverted pre-marital sex so bizarre that in her college days she could be sitting in class during a lecture and suddenly become overpowered by the smell of sex. She would feel the overwhelming urge to leave the class and find someone to sleep with, an urge she often gave in to.

As we began her deliverance, I handed her the egg. She took the egg and held it in the flat of her hand, palm up. We labored for hours, speaking to the spirits and commanding them to leave. While we experienced a level of success, seeing a number of the demons leave, it was obvious that we had been unable to locate the strongman. We directed our focus toward understanding more about the egg and at one point instructed Angel to break it open. A look of terror crossed her face and she recoiled as if to protect the egg. We commanded her in the name of Jesus to drop the egg and she let out an unearthly cackle and slowly but surely began to turn her hand that held the egg sitting on the flat of her palm.

The next series of events are astounding to me even until today, quite a few years after the event. Angel's hand rotated a full 180 degrees, but the egg would not drop. It appeared glued to her hand as she continued this demoniacal cackling. We began to command the egg to drop in the name of Jesus and just as suddenly as the cackling started, it stopped. She let out a piercing scream and dropped the egg. It shattered and splattered all over the floor, but to our amazement, didn't ooze yellow yolk but a blood red fluid.

Angel suddenly weakened visibly and could barely stand up on her feet. Suddenly one of the ministers received a clear revelation that the strongman was hiding in her feet. She immediately began to address it. Angel let out one final piercing scream and fell to the floor as rigid as if she were dead. Angel's deliverance had lasted all of four hours.

Incidentally, it was after Angel's deliverance that it became glaringly obvious to me that not only was it possible for Christians to have demons, but it was for Christians that Jesus introduced deliverance to the Church.

## Mike's miracle

Deliverance isn't always about dramatic rescues from the occult or from witchcraft. It isn't always about manifestations of rolling eyeballs, snaking tongues or convulsions. Deliverance is often to average people like you and I with average everyday struggles.

A friend of mine named Mike was the Children's Pastor at New Life Church in Colorado Springs when I first went on staff there in 1997. Shortly after Mike became a Christian in the late 1970s while in college in Missouri, he began to experience strange sensations and would sometimes see an evil-looking death mask offset slightly to the left of his head. It appeared almost real and really used to torment him.

He talked to one of the more mature Christian men about this, who explained deliverance to Mike and promptly offered to pray for him. As soon as he laid his hand on him, Mike felt something indescribable well up inside him and he began to experience a strange urge to want to choke the man to death. After they were done praying, Mike said it felt as if his insides had literally been scrubbed with a brush and this overwhelming sense of calm and cleanliness took over. However, this only lasted for about two weeks. Unfortunately, being the young Christian that he was, Mike had very little background in understanding deliverance and did not know that he was supposed to maintain it through prayer, the Word of God and continued confession of the Scriptures over himself.

He took a drastic turn for the worse as the demons came back with a vengeance. This time, he began to experience strong bouts of depression as well as suicidal thoughts. His present state was worse than his previous state before the deliverance (Luke 11:24-27). In further consultation with the brother who had prayed for him, he discovered what he was supposed to be doing to maintain his deliverance and went through the process again. This time it was with much more understanding and so he was able to maintain his deliverance and live victoriously over these previously destructive areas of his life.

## The "Ministry" of deliverance

There is a common misconception among Christians that deliverance is a special ministry, and that it is exclusively for those who are called to the ministry of deliverance. There is no biblical premise for either of these ideas. Deliverance is not identified anywhere in the Scriptures as a ministry the way we would identify the ministry of the pastor or teacher or the ministry of helps.

Also, the notion that deliverance is a special calling is quickly dispelled by the scriptures in Mark 16:17: "And these signs shall follow them that believe; In my name shall they cast out (demons) devils."

It is worthy of note that the Bible does not say these signs (the first of which is the ability to exorcise demons) shall follow pastors, apostles, prophets or people with a special calling. It simply says that "these signs shall follow them that believe." Clearly then, deliverance can be done by anyone in Church.

The fact that Christians shy away from deliverance serves to create an aura of mystique around it, further creating the mistaken impression that you have to be "called" in order to minister in deliverance. While I concede the fact that the more you do deliverance the greater your understanding of how to operate in that area, it is imperative to note that deliverance is no different from prayer or any other aspect of ministry. To become adept at prayer, you cannot read about prayer, you cannot attend conferences on prayer and you certainly cannot have others praying instead of you because you are not called to be an intercessor. If you want to become adept at prayer, you pray!

Like prayer, deliverance is a call to the entire Body of Christ. One way to remove the aura of mystique that surrounds it is by removing the special "ministry of deliverance" label that accompanies it, and encouraging more lay people to become involved.

At New Life Church, where I helped start the deliverance teams, they were made up primarily of people to whom I had ministered deliverance. I had made it a habit to explain that there were thousands of hurting Christians who needed deliverance, but too few people who were interested in getting involved in this area of ministry. I would encourage those I prayed for, saying that if they had received freedom from our ministry to them then it would be a good idea for them to get involved with us to help see other hurting Christians set free. When people have experienced freedom in Christ through deliverance, they tend to be more compassionate and sensitive to the needs of others in this area.

## "Come out!" "Come off!" "Get away!" (Which is it?)

Often as I have counseled with people prior to their deliverance, they have expressed confusion as to how a demon can be in them if, as the Bible teaches, they are filled with the Spirit of God. The often-asked question goes something like, "Is it in me, on me, around me…?"

In Luke 11:24-26, the Bible says:

> When an unclean spirit goes out of a man, he goes through dry places, seeking rest; and finding none, he says, 'I will return to my house from which I came.' And when he comes, he finds it swept and put in order. Then he goes and takes with him seven other spirits more wicked than himself, and they enter and dwell there; and the last state of that man is worse than the first."

Note that the phrase the Bible uses for the eviction of an unclean spirit is "goes out of a man." This literally means to depart from; proceed out of; escape out of.[1] In other words, the emphasis is on the fact of the demon first being in and then cast out. Because demons are disembodied spirits they are not constrained by size or space when they enter a person or an animal. In the story of the demoniac of the Gadarenes, it was the demons leaving the "insane" man and entering into the herd of swine that caused them to madly rush headlong into the sea and drown. (Luke 8: 26-33). In each case they were first in and then cast out.

Demons do not however, possess a person's spirit (except under extreme cases of Satanic ritual abuse, etc.), for, as earlier stated, they themselves are disembodied spirits. They only need a body to function through, so the argument as to whether or not Christians can be possessed is, in fact, a moot point. Further proof that demons do not possess people's spirits is in the fact that Jesus permitted them to go into the herd of swine. Animals do not have spirits; only humans are made in the image and likeness of God. The demons do not need a spirit to work through—they need a body. If they needed to possess a spirit then they would have been unable to enter into the herd of swine. Furthermore, the Bible teaches us in Mark 16:17 that in the name of Jesus, we shall cast out demons not cast off demons. You cannot cast out what is not within.

## Deliverance: Thanks but no thanks!

One of the most compassionate deliverance ministers I know is a woman I met years ago, to help her through her own deliverance. I became involved with her situation at the request of one of our church counselors who had been taking her through some emotional healing counseling. As they delved deep into her history at their counseling sessions, they discovered that there were ten years of her childhood that she could not recall. The counselor suggested that she visit with me and discuss the possibilities of going through some deliverance.

As she and I talked, I recognized some classic symptoms of abuse and fear that had caused her to block out those years from her memory in order to protect herself. Now, please understand that I am neither a psychiatrist nor a psychologist and am therefore not in the habit of diagnosing split personalities. I do, however, have the ability by the Spirit of God to recognize demonic influences, which were clearly at work here. We set up a time for her deliverance session.

In the meantime, I communicated with the counselor, who informed me that this lady was the owner of a fairly well-known business in town and was a little intimidated at the prospect of undergoing deliverance with all the possible manifestations.

On the morning of the deliverance, I met with the lady at the appointed time and couldn't help noticing how well dressed and proper she appeared. Every hair was in place and her dressing was impeccable. We began the deliverance session. Before long, she was gyrating and contorting all over the place. As we continued to address the demons, they began to manifest. Getting down on her hands and knees, she began to bark like a dog. We continued to address the spirits until we sensed a complete release and she was set free completely.

Prior to her deliverance, she had wanted nothing to do with deliverance. The mere mention of the word would send her running in the opposite direction. Today she is one of our more discerning ministers and is one of those who accompanies me every time we have to do ministry outside the church.

There is no doubt in my mind that in the midst of all the heavy theological debates as to the veracity of the doctrine of deliverance, once you've experienced freedom through the ministry of deliverance, all your skepticism is laid to rest.

## Many roads lead to freedom

Not long after I became a Christian, I was introduced to my first controversial dilemma. I was duly informed that deliverance was an area of ministry to stay away from as it was full of really "weird" people who lived with their heads perpetually in a spiritual cloud. I was informed that if I associated myself with such people, I would quickly be labeled one of them and would lose any measure of credibility I had as a well-rounded, balanced minister.

This was all well and good except for one small problem. Jesus had been involved in deliverance, ostensibly risking his entire ministry and reputation by allowing Himself to be identified with this previously unknown area of ministry. In addition to this more obvious fact, people really seemed to be experiencing freedom from various things that had bound them for so long prior to their deliverance.

You will always find excesses and abuses in any area of ministry that is subject to interpretation, as long as we are dealing with fallible humanity. This is not a valid reason to dispense with the aspects of truth that God has provided for His Church in order that we may walk in complete freedom. That would be throwing the proverbial baby out with the bath water.

I am truly grateful for people like Doris Wagner and their involvement in the ministry of deliverance. People like her nullify the argument that deliverance is an area of ministry full of "weirdoes". People like Doris remind you of Grandma next door. If Grandma is involved with deliverance, it can't be that bad and it certainly must be biblical. The method employed by Doris in doing deliverance differs from the method employed by Cleansing Stream Ministries, which in turn differs from the method that I have trained the New Life Church team to use. There is no doubt in my mind though, that each one of these methods, along with various others, are highly effective in seeing people set free from the bondage of the demonic. God is gracious and loves people more than methods. For this reason, He chooses to work through fallible human vessels despite our shortcomings as long as our motives are pure in wanting to see people set free.

# Origins of Demons

As a child, I was told that demons and ghosts were the restless spirits of dead people who had died prematurely. These people then hovered around as ghosts, ghouls and goblins until they could somehow complete their unfinished work. Apparently, I was not the only one sold this crock of lard, as evidenced by the popularity of the 1980's comedy "Ghostbusters," which recently enjoyed a revival on a special edition DVD. "Ghostbusters" is based on the lark that, if you have a ghost problem, you can just call 1-800-ZAP-A-GHOST. Before you can say, "Boo," they'll be at your door to suck up the slimy critters into a specially prepared, ghost-escape-proof bottle.

"Ghostbusters" is just one of a thousand examples of our people's current and past fascination with demons, ghosts and the occult. Over the centuries, humans have always been enthralled by the world of spirits. From the druids of medieval France to the mysteries of Stonehenge, from the zombies of South America to the witchdoctors of sub-Saharan Africa, dark spirituality has captivated the minds and hearts of countless individuals. More often than not, this fascination has devolved into shoddy thinking about the real presence of demons in the earth.

But ignorance, contrary to popular opinion, is not bliss. The world is in need of believable answers, and it's the responsibility of the Church to provide those answers. New age and Eastern mystic religions cannot provide adequate solutions to the spiritual needs of our day. It is therefore incumbent upon the Church to provide the truth as the Scriptures portray it.

The Bible says, "You shall know the truth and the truth shall set you free." The Greek word translated "know" is from the root word epignosis[1], which means to experience, to have intimate knowledge of. We need to know the truth deeply. This is my prayer for you as we, together, explore the biblical origin of demons.

## Biblical references to Satan

A few years ago, I had the opportunity to speak at the first International Congress on Deliverance hosted by Dr. C. Peter Wagner's Global Harvest Ministries in Colorado Springs, Colorado. Well over three thousand people attended the conference, many of whom probably knew more about deliverance than I did.

A few weeks after the conference, I received a package in the mail from a gentleman (we will call him Alex) based in Washington. Alex graciously sent me a book he had written and self-published along with a rather thoughtful letter explaining to me that, with regard to the origin of demons, I was erroneously teaching traditional, extra-biblical myths. He made it quite clear that he was not sending me the book to persuade me to change my mind, "but to offer an alternate opinion based on what the Bible really does tell us."

Bless his dear heart, but Alex's book hasn't convinced me that I am in error regarding the origin of demons. Since his primary contention is a popular one, let's look at it in detail.

Alex's main concern was with the interpretation of Isaiah 14: 3, 4, 12-17:

> It shall come to pass in the day the Lord gives you rest from your sorrow, and from your fear and the hard bondage in which you were made to serve, that you will take up this proverb

> against the king of Babylon, and say: "How the oppressor has ceased, the golden city ceased! How you are fallen from heaven, O Lucifer, son of the morning! How you are cut down to the ground, you who weakened the nations! For you have said in your heart: 'I will ascend into heaven, I will exalt my throne above the stars of God; I will also sit on the mount of the congregation on the farthest sides of the north; I will ascend above the heights of the clouds, I will be like the Most High.' Yet you shall be brought down to Sheol, to the lowest depths of the Pit. Those who see you will gaze at you, and consider you, saying: 'Is this the man who made the earth tremble, who shook kingdoms, who made the world as a wilderness and destroyed its cities, who did not open the house of his prisoners?'"

It is commonly accepted in charismatic circles that the reference to Lucifer here is a reference to Satan and his expulsion from heaven. But Alex suggests that this is a misrepresentation of the truth. He cites Luther, Calvin and Clarke as reputable Bible scholars who decry this application. Alex states in his book,

> In the Bible, there is no pre-Adamic earth, no Angel of light called Lucifer, no satanic rebellion and banishment…in the Bible, Satan has never been a covering cherub or a glorious and revered ruling being; he has never been a third archangel along with Michael and Gabriel; he has never been creation's leader of worship. In the Bible, Satan was never perfect in all his ways until iniquity was found in him; he was never lifted up with pride to covet heaven's throne; he never fell from an original innocence.

But Luther, Calvin, and Clarke are missing an important point: the Bible does indeed say that Satan fell from heaven. In Luke 10:18, Jesus states, "I saw Satan fall like lightning from heaven," suggesting that he did indeed fall from innocence and that Isaiah 14 is a reference to this fall. Another biblical reference to this fall is found in Ezekiel 28, which reads:

> You were the seal of perfection, full of wisdom and perfect in beauty. You were in Eden, the garden of God; every precious stone was your covering: the sardius, topaz, and diamond,

> beryl, onyx, and jasper, sapphire, turquoise, and emerald with gold. The workmanship of your timbrels and pipes was prepared for you on the day you were created. "You were the anointed cherub who covers; established you; you were on the holy mountain of God; you walked back and forth in the midst of fiery stones. You were perfect in your ways from the day you were created, till iniquity was found in you. By the abundance of your trading you became filled with violence within, and you sinned; therefore I cast you as a profane thing out of the mountain of God; and I destroyed you, O covering cherub, from the midst of the fiery stones. Your heart was lifted up because of your beauty; you corrupted your wisdom for the sake of your splendor; I cast you to the ground, I laid you before kings, that they might gaze at you. You defiled your sanctuaries by the multitude of your iniquities, by the iniquity of your trading; therefore I brought fire from your midst; it devoured you, and I turned you to ashes upon the earth in the sight of all who saw you. All who knew you among the peoples are astonished at you; you have become a horror, and shall be no more forever.

Furthermore, Satan's appearance in the Garden of Eden in the form of a serpent to tempt the woman to rebel against God is not left to conjecture, and Satan is again well identified for us in Revelation 20: 2. If Satan was in the Garden of Eden and he also appeared before God in the book of Job along with the other angels, wouldn't common sense dictate that when Ezekiel and Isaiah reference an anointed Cherub that was in the Garden of Eden, it would be Satan, and not Adam?

Apart from these biblical references, we have another perfectly good reason to believe that Satan fell from heaven. In order for God to devise His elaborate scheme of salvation to rescue man from the jaws of death, there had to be a reason for rescue. If God is not the author of evil—and according to the Bible God only makes good and perfect things—then He could not have created Satan in the way that he exists now, as Satan represents the antithesis of all that is good. So, Satan must have been an angel of light who willfully rejected God.

In fact, the Bible is replete with clear references to Satan and his demons. There is simply no getting around the issue.

## Of Men and Giants

The story of demons begins as far back as Genesis. God is very pleased with the world He has created, and is especially pleased with His creation of man. But by chapter six, God is singing to a different tune because of the infiltration of the pure seed of humanity by a root of evil.

The Bible says that in those days when the sons of men had daughters, the sons of God took them as wives:

> Now it came to pass, when men began to multiply on the face of the earth, and daughters were born to them, that the sons of God saw the daughters of men, that they were beautiful; and they took wives for themselves of all whom they chose. And the Lord said, "My Spirit shall not strive with man forever, for he is indeed flesh; yet his days shall be one hundred and twenty years." There were giants on the earth in those days, and also afterward, when the sons of God came in to the daughters of men and they bore children to them. Those were the mighty men who were of old, men of renown.
>
> Then the Lord saw that the wickedness of man was great in the earth, and that every intent of the thoughts of his heart was only evil continually. And the Lord was sorry that He had made man on the earth, and He was grieved in His heart.

## Genesis 6: 1 – 6

Now, the word for "sons of God" in this passage is the same word used elsewhere to signify angels. In other words, the relations described here were between human women and fallen angels. According to the Bible, through these mixed marriages came a strange race of beings called the giants, or nephilim (the race from which Goliath of Gath descended). Subsequent to this corruption of human seed, the thoughts and intents of man's heart became continually evil. Where man had previously exercised his conscience in deciding between right and wrong, now he continually exercised it for evil—so much so, in fact, that God was saddened that he had made man.

What caused the change? Why would people who had previously demonstrated such a desire for fellowship with God suddenly make a dramatic turn and align themselves as the adversary of God? Was this a new, more sinful race? And how had they come to be?

The answer lies back in the Garden of Eden. After the fall, Satan began looking for a way to break God's curse against him. You see, after Satan had tempted the woman and caused her and her husband to eat of the forbidden fruit, God placed a curse on the serpent condemning him to eat dust and crawl upon his belly all of his days. God also assured him that the seed of the woman would ultimately bruise his head (Genesis 3:14-15). In other words, God was telling the serpent that it would have to struggle against people throughout the course of history and ultimately suffer defeat at the hands of humanity.

But Satan was looking for a loophole. If there was one thing he knew for sure, it was that God would never establish intimacy with "contaminated" seed. Satan knew that a holy God could not be in the presence of sin, so he thought if he could corrupt the seed of the woman, God would be unable to use her seed to destroy him. Satan determined that if he could infiltrate the seed of woman and corrupt their consciences by breeding his demonic horde of fallen angels with the daughters of men, he would transmogrify all of humanity.

This demonic horde of angels is not mentioned in the creation narrative in Genesis, but we know a legion of angels existed before the creation of humans and that some of those angels rejected God (again, this is the action referred to in Ezekiel 28). So, when Satan wanted to entice man into his rebellion against God, he had his demonic hordes take on the form of attractive men and seduce the human women. The result of these unholy unions was the nephilim.

## The Dispensation of Conscience

In order to understand why Satan chose this tactic, to crossbreed humanity with his demonic hordes and consequently release a plague of demons upon the earth, we must understand how God deals with man in dispensations. Bible Scholars agree that there are seven dispensations in which God has dealt with or will deal with man. They are: innocence; conscience; human government; law; prophets; grace; and the millennial kingdom.[2] When God first created Adam and Eve to tend the Garden of Eden, they lived in what Bible scholars have come to refer to as the dispensation of innocence. It has been so named because they lived in blissful ignorance of evil and so were even unaware of their nakedness, or at least unashamed of it. Even though they had access to the tree of the knowledge of good and evil, they were forbidden to partake of its fruit.

After they fell to the temptation of the serpent, they were banished from the Garden so that they wouldn't eat of the tree of life and live forever in their fallen, sinful state. At this juncture God begins to deal with them based on the dictates of their conscience since they now had the capacity to choose between good and evil. This period is referred to as the dispensation of conscience.

Back at the Garden, Satan tempted Eve to rebel against God by assuring her that the only reason God had instructed them not to eat of the tree of the knowledge of good and evil was because He didn't want them to become like God, knowing all things. Satan, since his banishment from heaven, had taken upon himself the unenviable responsibility of enticing God's creation away from Him. Because his initial rebellion was successful only in removing him from the presence of God, he devised a plan to seduce the most precious of God's creation, Mankind. This is what he still attempts to do today. In identifying this fact, John, in the tenth chapter of his gospel states that the thief (Satan) has come only to steal, to kill and to destroy. The simple but not always obvious plan of the devil is to stir up rebellion in our hearts so that we become ostracized from God. This is why the influence of demons upon mankind is such a vital part of the devil's plan to distort the purpose of God for the Church.

He reckoned without Jesus as he concocted his diabolical plan.

## Ghostbusters or Demonbusters?

In understanding this, one can see the rationale behind the dubious but seemingly effective plan of Satan's attempt to distort humanity by creating a corrupt seed. I say seemingly effective because he reckoned without his Maker's wisdom. God sent Jesus as a pure, uncorrupted seed to be born of a woman, who would in the very sacrifice of his life for humanity fulfill God's plan to have the seed of the woman bruise the head of the serpent. In the course of his temptation and the fall of mankind, Satan also usurped man's God-given authority to have dominion over the earth and consequently became the god of this world (II Corinthians 4: 4). The plan is still the same today: control the hearts and minds of men and cause them to reject God's rule and authority through the influence of demons so that they become subject to his dominion in their fallen sinful state.

The good news is that we can know with full confidence where demons come from. There need be no mystery about their origin and we don't need to be stupidly fascinated in a "Ghostbusters" or "Tales from the crypt" sort of way. We can be intelligent, confident and forthright in our dealings with demons and confront them with a biblical foundation of truth and a spiritual precedent in power.

# Power in the Blood

While in college in the early 1980's, I joined a notorious organization known as the Pyrates Confraternity. At my school, the very mention of this group struck terror in the hearts of other students. It was common knowledge that when the Pyrates were out "sailing," if you valued your life you would make sure that you were locked safely indoors. The image of the Pyrates was one of devil worshipping, alcohol drinking, and pot smoking evil men. If they were around, you wanted to be anywhere else.

Over the years, the line between truth and myth had blurred, and the Pyrates were reputed to drink blood during their late night ritualistic celebrations. This, though far from being true, was only one of dozens of bizarre perceptions that the public held of this cult, many of which were true.

Membership in this exclusive, esoteric fraternity was limited to a very select few who had proven themselves capable by going through the most exacting initiation rites. As new initiates, you selected new names that symbolized your new life. Names such as Judas Christ, Jesus Iscariot, Gravedigger, Death Angel and others were not uncommon and were certainly preferred to milder names like Broken Bones, Seagull and Bloody Nemesis. The more devious the name, the more rugged you were said to be.

Once a name was chosen, your pact with the brotherhood was ratified in blood. A scroll was prepared with the new names of all the initiates added to it (the names of all other existing members would already be on the scroll). One by one, you would be called forward by the Capone (head of the organization) and one of your fingers would be cut. The blood from your finger would then be allowed to drip onto the scroll beside your name. This final rite of initiation ensured that you were now a member of a brotherhood whose covenant and commitment was stronger than that which you share with your own fraternal sibling. The Capone was the keeper of the scroll and he guarded and valued it as his most sacred possession.

By now, you're seeing the obvious and eerie comparisons between the Pyrates Confraternity and Christianity. The new birth. The scroll or Book of Life. Membership into a special, close-knit family. And, most strikingly, a covenant established through blood.

Blood has played a role in covenants and rituals throughout human history. The Old Testament is replete with examples of blood sacrifices of bulls, goats and birds, all serving to atone for the sins of the people. Each year, the high priest would enter the Holy of Holies once a year to offer sacrifice on behalf of himself and the entire nation to ensure that their relationship with God continued to be viable. The shed blood of the sacrificial animal would serve as a covering for their sins and allow them to enjoy the blessings of a covenant relationship with God for another year.

The power of a blood covenant is also demonstrated through the story of Abram. Even before God had made him the father of a multitude of nations, Abram knew that the promise of God to him was as good as money in the bank. He agreed to leave the security of Ur of the Chaldees (Mesopotamia) and head towards the Promised Land based on this word from God:

> I will make you a great nation;
>
> I will bless you and make your name great;

And you shall be a blessing.

-Genesis 12: 2

But to Abram's thinking, God was a little slow in bringing on the blessing. Upon arrival in Canaan, Abram began to fret just a bit and even tried to twist God's arm into hurrying the process of fulfilling His promise. "Sarai's biological clock is ticking," he reminded God. Abram complained that the only heir in his house was Eliezer of Damascus, and if he was going to be a great progenitor, he desperately needed some progeny!

God was evidently not in as much of a rush as Abram was, as Isaac was born 25 years after his arrival in the Promised Land. When that happened, the covenant was sealed through the shedding of blood in circumcision.

The power of the blood is incomparable in its ability to seal covenants and cleanse sin. From the beginning of time, God saw fit to establish blood as a sign of atonement and a propitiation for sin. Abel's sacrifice was more acceptable than Cain's was because he shed the blood of a lamb as an offering to God. This was a type of Christ, whose blood would be shed for the redemption of mankind. Hebrews 9:22 says, "Without shedding of blood there is no remission." And Leviticus 17: 11 says, "For the life of the flesh is in the blood, and I have given it to you upon the altar to make atonement for your souls; for it is the blood that makes atonement for the soul."

Little wonder then, that Satan would seek to corrupt this symbol. Through various means, Satan has always sought to contaminate the blood covenant. It is for this reason that the Pyrates Confraternity saw fit to unwittingly seal brotherhood pacts in blood. It is for this reason that the god Molech required the blood sacrifice of innocent children, and it is for this same reason that the modern day practice of satanic ritual abuse requires the shedding of innocent blood to seal the terms of their covenant. Satan's recognition of the power of the shed blood of Christ on the cross and its ability to redeem motivates him to require worship and blood sacrifices as a counterfeit king.

Of course, there is still power in the blood today, and I've discovered that one of the most effective weapons for pulling down satanic strongholds is the blood of Jesus Christ. From the Abrahamic to the Davidic covenants, from the priesthood of Zechariah to the priesthoods of Annas and Caiaphas, they knew the shedding of blood was required for atonement. But Christ came, "...as high priest of the good things that are already here...he did not enter by means of the blood of goats and calves; but he entered the Most Holy Place once for all by his own blood, having obtained eternal redemption" (Hebrews 9: 11,12 NIV).

Max Lucado calls this positional sanctification.[1] The effects of the shed blood of Jesus are accredited to us, cleansing us from all sin and eliminating the need to pay further price for our sin. The victims of satanic ritual abuse have been sealed in blood covenants with Satan through ritual sacrifices. Those covenants are negated once and for all through acceptance of the finished work of Christ on the cross. The reason that the blood of Jesus carries such authority is because He paid a grievous price by dying in place of sinful man. There is no longer need for further blood sacrifices. Acceptance of His shed blood provides you access to the promises of the new covenant and destroys the power of any previous covenant. It is in just the same way that it eliminated the need for (or effects of) the high priest entering into the Holy of Holies once a year to make atonement for the sins of the people. As I pray with victims of satanic ritual abuse, I tell them that they are now sealed under a stronger covenant than any that they entered into previously and they are therefore no longer beholden to the devil and his works of darkness.

## Two Blood Sacrifices

The Pyrates Confraternity (PC) was loosely modeled after the legendary swarthy buccaneers such as Peg-leg Pete and Captain Hook. In my first year as a new initiate, we were referred to as deckhands and literally were to be seen and not heard. This was a particularly trying period, as it was designed to slowly but surely break down your sense of individuality. You could no longer think for yourself, but were simply a small part of a huge organism.

We were summoned at random at all hours of the day or night to carry out menial chores for the older "seadogs." The decision to join the Pyrates cost you the chance to choose your own friends; it was an organization that required the utmost loyalty. This meant that if at any time you were determined to be spending more time with "landlubbers" than with your fellow seadogs, you were apt to be disciplined. These unwritten rules and regulations that guided our lives transcended the campus environment as the organization stretched far beyond the walls of the universities.

By the time I joined the PC, it had been in existence for almost thirty years. Professor Wole Soyinka, Nigeria's Nobel Prize winner for literature, as a modern day Robin Hood movement, defending the downtrodden and defenseless, had started it. Somewhere along the way, the lines had blurred and the Pyrates had developed a reputation for being thugs and hooligans. On numerous university campuses, they had been banned and thus operated illegally as an "underground" organization.

I'm giving you a behind-the-scenes peek, but there are numerous people today who have nothing but good to say about the Pyrates Confraternity. Even though over time some questionable characters had joined the organization and some dubious rituals had begun, the large majority of us still believed in the original ideals of the organization and were seen as somewhat of an unofficial campus police force, quickly dispensing justice and keeping the peace.

One of these good young men who were in the PC for the right reasons was "Andy." Andy had come from a school that was a pre-university preparatory college (one of very few in Nigeria) and the only school other than a university that had a branch of the Pyrates Confraternity. Andy had been the Capone there and so was a seasoned veteran by the time he came to our university.

I was a deckhand the year he came. Because Andy had so much stature from his previous position of authority, we were in the awkward position of referring to two different people as Capone that year. Inevitably, two different factions began to emerge and it slowly became obvious that there was a slight tussle for power.

As a deckhand, we had no powers whatsoever and even though the constitution of the PC called for a two-thirds majority in the event of a mutiny to overthrow the sitting Capone, deckhands did not have a vote. So, the night that the rebelling faction called an emergency deck meeting, I was not invited. The events of that evening were reported to me secondhand, but I will recount them as best as I can.

Andy and a few dissenters had decided that they were going to take power from the sitting Capone, as he was perceived as too soft, too involved with landlubbers and definitely not rugged enough to be Capone. Unfortunately, some of them had broken ranks and had leaked word of the meeting so that the sitting Capone had gotten wind of it. He sent his High Priest to the meeting, a rather psychologically disturbed individual who was feared by almost everyone because of his known erratic behavior and his ability to inflict harm on someone at the slightest perception of disrespect or disloyalty.

When he arrived to break up the mutiny, a scuffle ensued. During the fight, he brought out a dagger and stabbed Andy, wounding him severely. Andy was rushed to the local teaching hospital, where a story was concocted that he had been hurt in an alcohol-induced fight in which the culprit had stabbed him and then disappeared. Andy's wounds proved fatal and the capabilities of the medical staff at the hospital proved inadequate. Andy died around 2:00 a.m. that morning.

The next few hours were a flurry of activity. All deckhands were woken from sleep at 3:00 a.m. for an emergency meeting. We were informed of the tragic events and told to stick by the drunken brawl story. But it wasn't long before the truth came out and the police became involved.

All the spinning and truth twisting in the world could not stop the avalanche of rage that ensued following the disclosure of Andy's untimely and pointless death. Andy was just 20 or 21-years-old when he died. A promising life cut short. A futile effort to preserve an already crusty tradition of machismo. Was it worth it? What did Andy's death leave behind other than a legacy evidencing the flaw of human character? The killer got away with it. He was from a wealthy family and so his parents' influence got him a slap on the wrist and a transfer to a foreign country to finish his schooling. Andy died needlessly and without justice with the promise of yet unborn children still in his loins. Some precious young lady somewhere was deprived of the opportunity to grow old with Andy. Innocent blood spilled in vain.

And the Pyrates Confraternity? A mere shadow of its former self. It was unable to continue in its noble traditions and ideals after the priceless sacrifice of a precious human life.

As I've learned since, Andy's death is a perfect corollary to Jesus' sacrificial death on the cross…

Satan planned a mutiny in the Garden of Eden along with a third of the Angels. His objective? To unseat the King of kings. The reason? Jesus was too kind, too concerned about His created beings. He wasn't rugged enough to be king. Like so many deckhands who weren't quite clued in, humanity was the unwitting accomplice to a mutiny.

But unlike Andy's, Jesus' blood was not shed in vain. In His death, victory for all mankind was assured. The Bible says, "Having disarmed principalities and powers, He made a public spectacle of them, triumphing over them in it" (Colossians 4: 3). In the shedding of His blood, Jesus knew that the battle for the souls of humanity would be won and all the plans of the devil would be rendered impotent.

For the believer, this is where the power and the victory lie: at the cross, where the Blood of God completed the work of salvation for all mankind.

## The Blood of God

The road is never ending, paved with the dust of a thousand Middle Eastern summers. Still He trudges on wearily, the weight of the world resting upon His shoulders. Women weep by the wayside, reaching out to Him as if a touch from them will take away the pain. Men are visibly shaken and struggle to keep their emotions in check as they watch the forlorn figure stumble under the weight of the cross. Their cross!

Jesus was born to die. Imagine that! Imagine being born knowing that the world can only be made better by your death. What an enormous load to bear, knowing that your path is predetermined and your destiny is to die for the sins of mankind. And what a death. Crucifixion! The worst possible death in Roman-ruled Palestine. Crucifixion was reserved for the vilest offenders in society. Hung upon a cross in full view of the entire city, to be ridiculed, scorned, spat upon and stoned at will.

Death by crucifixion not only carried with it the stigma of shame, but the condemned man also suffered hours of excruciating pain and eventually died by suffocation. Why did God choose this method of death for His Son? Why couldn't He have died a more respectable death? If I knew the answers to these and many other questions surrounding His death, I would be as omniscient as God is. I can speculate, however, that in order for the sins of mankind to be paid in full (the wages of sin is death), Jesus had to experience the shame that the vilest, basest person on earth would have experienced. Quite possibly, if Jesus had walked the earth today, He may have subjected Himself to death by lethal injection, the electric chair or some other such objectionable form of death.

## Applying the Blood

Because of the work of the redeeming nature of the blood that was shed on Calvary, during deliverance we pray a blood covering around the ministry team as well as the ones being ministered to. We invite the Holy Spirit's presence through a time of prayer and worship preparatory to the actual time of ministry. Each member of the ministry team is anointed with oil (typifying the Holy Spirit). I then pray a specific prayer asking for a hedge of the blood of Jesus to surround them as a protective covering.

During the actual time of ministry; we pray specific scriptures identifying the power in the shed blood of Jesus. We address the demons in the name of Jesus and remind them of the completed work of the cross and how the blood of Jesus was shed on Calvary, triumphing over every work of darkness. We lead the person being ministered to in a prayer nullifying the powers of demonic strongholds in their lives and identifying the blood of Jesus as having brought them victory. We refer to this process as "pleading the blood."

After the time of personal ministry, we provide them with information that we have put together identifying how they are to maintain their deliverance through prayer and the study of the scriptures. As part of the process we encourage them to pray a blood covering over themselves and their families daily.

# Understanding the Occult

The two women at the table are shrouded in an eerie glow. One woman's face bears anxious anticipation, the other's is a study in deep concentration: eyes closed, deep furrows etched across her brow. Softly, we hear a slight rustling of the drapes. Then the noise intensifies, followed by a loud rushing wind. Suddenly the woman at the head of the table bolts upright, her eyes open wide as saucers. She shoots straight up out of her chair and with an unblinking, dazed look heads straight towards the kitchen.

The woman still sitting at the table remains motionless. Tentatively, she asks, "Harold, Harold is that you?" Without acknowledging the question, the other woman continues marching straight into the kitchen, opens the refrigerator, and marches back out with a bottle of beer in one hand while the other hand liberally eases the discomfort of an itch in her gluteus maximus.

She walks into the living room, grabs the TV remote control and promptly plunks herself down in front of a football game. With a smile of dawning recognition, the other woman reaches her arms out, cooing, "Harold!"

Sound like fiction? It is. This was a national advertising campaign run for a beer product. What's happening is obvious, but let's unpack it a little further.

One of these women has decided to consult with her dear departed husband, Harold, through the use of a medium. The séance begins with the medium attempting to contact Harold by allowing herself to be used as a channel. The sound of the wind blowing, along with the sudden change in the medium's countenance, indicates the presence of Harold in the room, who then enters the medium's body. Still a little unsure, the woman tentatively calls out her husband's name. She continues to observe "his" activities as he operates through the medium. Confirmation that the awakened spirit of Harold has now possessed the medium is finally assured when "he" does all the familiar things that he did when he was alive: "He" gets a beer out of the refrigerator, scratches "himself" indiscreetly, and proceeds to the TV to watch a game of football, totally ignoring "his" wife's presence. With a smile of recognition, she acknowledges him by calling his name.

There are enough subtle negative messages in this advertisement to warrant an entire dissertation. But for our purposes, the point is this: our culture is increasingly open to the occult. Light-hearted advertisements like this, as well as movies, television shows, and popular music are often filled with occult images and themes. Satan knows how to disguise his schemes. Once these types of things become acceptable in our culture, we become desensitized to the underlying spirits at work. If we allow our society to imbibe these messages, we unwittingly provide the platform that Satan needs to launch an all-out attack against our values and our moral standards as dictated by the word of God.

The Bible takes this subject seriously, so we must take it seriously, too. Leviticus 19:31 says, "Give no regard to mediums and familiar spirits; do not seek after them, to be defiled by them: I am the Lord your God." Similarly, in Deuteronomy 18:10-12 we are told that "there shall not be found among you anyone…who conjures spells, or a medium, or a spiritist, or one who calls up the dead. For all who do these things are an abomination to the Lord."

Also, I Samuel 28:3 – 20 relates the story of Saul's encounter with the witch of Endor. Saul is on a quest to find out his destiny as well as answers to some troubling questions he has. Knowing that the witch of Endor is a medium who can channel spirits of the dead, he seeks her out to help him revive the spirit of Samuel the prophet, who is dead. This singular act of disobedience by Saul leads to his ultimate demise.

In short, the occult is no joke.

## Identifying the occult

But what exactly is the occult? And how do we recognize it when we see it?

Deuteronomy 18:9-14 lists some basic occult practices, all of which are common and widespread today:

> When you come into the land which the Lord your God is giving you, you shall not learn to follow the abominations of those nations. There shall not be found among you anyone who makes his son or his daughter pass (be sacrificed as an offering to an idol) through the fire, or one who practices witchcraft, or a soothsayer, or one who interprets omens, or a sorcerer, or one who conjures spells, or a medium, or a spiritist, or one who calls up the dead. For all who do these things are an abomination to the Lord, and because of these abominations the Lord your God drives them out from before you. You shall be blameless before the Lord your God. For these nations which you will dispossess listened to soothsayers and diviners; but as for you, the Lord your God has not appointed such for you.

Here, the following are specifically identified as occult practices: child sacrifice (Satanic Ritual Abuse, more commonly identified as SRA); divination; astrology; mediums; witchcraft; necromancy. Each one of these practices has a modern day application or parallel.

## Child sacrifice

This is undoubtedly one of the most horrific levels of human depravity. The very idea of an innocent child being sacrificed to idols to feed some demon's insatiable appetite for blood is reprehensible.

Leviticus 18:21 says, "Do not give any of your children to be sacrificed to Molech, for you must not profane the name of your God. I am the Lord." Molech was the chief deity of the Amalekites, a people who were constantly at war with Israel. The name "Molech," according to *Strong's Exhaustive Concordance of the Bible*, means to reign or ascend the throne.[1] This represents a type of the world system of evil that has aligned itself against God's rule and authority, as well as against his people. The Amalekites are a symbol of our constant battle against the occult and the dominion of the demonic. Molech represents the ruling spiritual deity that seeks to control the Amalekites through fear and bondage—he required ritual child sacrifices of the Amalekites in order to offer them protection and help them obtain victory in battle.

One of the most widely accepted extra-biblical chronicles of the history of the Jews is the writings of Flavius Josephus. Josephus was born of Jewish ancestry as Joseph ben Matthias, and later became a Roman citizen, chronicling Rome's military exploits. After Titus had overrun Jerusalem in 70 A.D., Josephus wrote *The Antiquities of The Jews* to recount the history. This is what he had to say concerning the Amalekites with reference to the Lord's directive to King Saul:

> I enjoin thee to punish the Amalekites, by making war upon them, and when thou hast subdued them, to leave none of them alive, but to pursue them through every age, and to slay them, beginning with the women and the infants, and to require this as a punishment to be inflicted upon them for the mischief they did to our forefathers: to spare nothing, neither asses nor other beasts; nor to reserve any of them for your own advantage and possession, but to devote them universally to God, and, in obedience to the commands of Moses, to blot out the name of Amalek entirely…for God hated the nation of the Amalekites to such a degree, that he commanded Saul to have no pity on even those infants which we by nature chiefly compassionate; but Saul preserved their king and governor from the miseries which the Hebrews brought on the people, as if he preferred

the fine appearance of the enemy to the memory of what God had sent him about."[2]

This is a clear type of God warning His people that the occult (worship of false gods; esoteric religions) would be an enemy that they would have to battle "through all ages" and that to compromise their values by allowing it to happen under their noses would spell imminent destruction.

Our generation has indeed compromised these values. When we are open to psychic hotlines, commercials that promote sorcery, overt and blatant witchcraft, and Satanism (to name a few) all in the name of religious freedom, then we are no doubt in danger of drawing the ire of the Lord down upon us. And it's not just in jokey commercials and sitcoms that these things exist: the ritual sacrificing of children is not uncommon in our society and has become a mainstay of Satanic Ritual Abuse.

## Satanic ritual abuse

At the World Congress on Deliverance in July of 1999, I met with a pastor and his wife who had been ministering to a young lady with an intense case of SRA. The young lady (we will call her Marie) had been raised in a satanic cult to which her parents belonged. As a child, she had witnessed the ritual sacrifice of a baby, and she had been used for perverted sexual gratification for some of their dark, bizarre rituals until she was old enough to make a choice to leave the cult. Of course, this had scarred her deeply and had left her feeling hopeless.

These precious pastors had taken her under their wing and were determined to see her set free. When I first met Marie, I was struck by how devoid of emotion she appeared. We spent hours working with Marie with little success. After the conference, I determined to find out more about SRA victims and how to go about doing deliverance on such people. The chapter dealing with blood covering and generational curses will address this subject in depth.

There is no doubt that one of the reasons the United States of America is such a great nation is due to its diversity and freedom of choice. There is, however, a lack of wisdom as well as a display of spiritual tyranny in the proliferation of spiritual matter in this nation. We are open to everything, including Satanism, meaning we are also open to the demonically inspired practice of ritualistic child sacrifices. Ironically, this constitutes a lack of true spiritual freedom ("You shall know the truth and the truth will set you free," reads John 8: 32).

## Divination

Divination is another misunderstood occult practice. Go to any state fair, circus or theme park today, and you are almost guaranteed to find the inevitable fortunetellers booth, complete with its "eastern" mystic ambience, its crystal ball and tarot cards along with all the other necessary paraphernalia for divining the future.

By definition, divination is the art or practice of using omens or magic powers to foretell the future. Our world is obsessed with the desire to see into the future. The Bible is clear on this issue: Fortune telling (divination) is demonically inspired. Only God is omniscient (possessing infinite awareness, understanding and insight). Satan counterfeits real spiritual gifts. In the book of I Corinthians 12: 8, the word of wisdom and the word of knowledge are listed as spiritual gifts. According to Dr. Lester Sumrall, the word of wisdom is the ability to supernaturally foretell an event before it occurs.[3]

In his book, The Holy Spirit and His Gifts, Kenneth E. Hagin defines words of wisdom as supernatural revelations by the Spirit of God concerning the divine purpose and plan in the mind and will of God. The word of knowledge is the ability to supernaturally receive information about a person or event.[4] All of these gifts are divinely inspired and are always for the purpose of glorifying God and demonstrating His omnipotence. Satan's counterfeits, on the other hand are an attempt to align himself with God through deception, to induce you to think that they are all a manifestation of God's spiritual gifts.

Ask yourself the question: Have you ever seen a counterfeit $7.00 bill? I am fairly certain your answer is "no," because there are no real $7.00 bills in circulation. Satan is more effective in his deception when his counterfeits resemble the real thing.

Consider the following story in the Acts 16:16-19:

> Now it happened, as we went to prayer, that a certain slave girl possessed with a spirit of divination met us, who brought her masters much profit by fortune-telling. This girl followed Paul and us, and cried out, saying, "These men are the servants of the Most High God, who proclaim to us the way of salvation."
>
> And this she did for many days. But Paul, greatly annoyed, turned and said to the spirit, "I command you in the name of Jesus Christ to come out of her." And he came out that very hour. But when her masters saw that their hope of profit was gone, they seized Paul and Silas and dragged them into the marketplace to the authorities.

Fascinating story! The first question that springs to my mind, though, is: why on earth did Paul cast out the spirit? After all, she was speaking the truth. What better way to reveal the power of God than to have demons also acknowledging Him?

Satan's counterfeits seek to align themselves with God. The demon of divination working through the girl knew that Paul and Silas were only in town for a short while. It also knew (as all demons do), that the Spirit of God was working through these men with miraculous signs and wonders. What better way to deceive people than to align itself with them for the period of time that they were in town? After they left, imagine how good business would be, especially among Christians, since they would have seen the spirit identifying with Paul and Silas. This was no word of knowledge gift in operation. Paul sought once and for all to expose the schemes of Satan by exposing this clairvoyant for what she was—a counterfeit.

This obsession with being able to see into the future transcends just psychic cognition. Horoscopes, tarot cards, palm reading, Ouija boards, ESP (extra sensory perception), astral projection, yoga, new age and eastern "mind developing" religions are all part of an endless list. All of these practices have not only become acceptable, but are the norm in today's society. Hollywood and professional sports boast celebrities who have "found inner peace" while on pilgrimages to the Far East seeking spiritual enlightenment. For those who can't afford the time or expense involved in one of those enlightenment trips, yoga, or any one of the numerous eastern mystic religions, are now available right here on our doorstep.

Many of our daily newspapers syndicate horoscope columns to tell you what the solar system's current alignment has to say about your future. Tarot cards and Ouija boards are available at almost any store—in the toy section, no less. And you can stop in at the nearest funfair or traveling circus to have your palm read by a resident fortune-teller. All this in a society that at one time professed to be essentially Christian. What must this do to the heart of God, knowing that He has warned us explicitly against such practices?

## Astrology

*Webster's New World Dictionary of the American Language* defines astrology as "a pseudo-science claiming to foretell the future by the supposed influence of the stars, planets, etc., on human affairs."

Read what the Bible has to say about astrology.

> Keep on, then, with your magic spells and with your many sorceries, which you have labored at since childhood. Perhaps you will succeed, perhaps you will cause terror. All the counsel you have received has only worn you out! *Let your astrologers come forward, those stargazers who make predictions month by month*, let them save you from what is coming upon you. Surely they are like stubble; the fire will burn them up. They cannot even save themselves from the power of the flame. Here are no coals to warm any one; here is no fire to sit by.
>
> That is all they can do for you—these you have labored with and trafficked with since childhood. Each of them goes on in his error; there is not one that can save you. - Isaiah 47: 12 – 15 (NIV)

By divine insight, Agabus received a revelation of what Paul would encounter when he reached Jerusalem. Acts 21:10 –11 (NIV) reads,

"After we had been there a number of days, a prophet named Agabus came down from Judea. Coming over to us, he took Paul's belt, tied his own hands and feet with it and said, 'The Holy Spirit says, "In this way the Jews of Jerusalem will bind the owner of this belt and will hand him over to the gentiles."

The devil has sought to make a mockery of this gift of revelation through the use of divination, astrology and the consulting of mediums. Plainly, God does not desire for us to turn to the stars or any other heavenly body to seek answers for the future. He has provided in His word all that pertains to life and godliness. As He sees fit, He causes the supernatural to intersect with the natural and divulges a word of wisdom or a prophecy, giving us divine insight into the future.

## Mediums

Many years ago when I lived in Lagos, Nigeria I had an interesting encounter with a medium. My mother had determined that a lot of the problems I was dealing with were of a spiritual nature and so she arranged for me to visit with a spiritist who would supposedly take care of all my problems once and for all. I drove to the man's home one afternoon and he directed me to a room that he had prepared for our "prayer" time.

On the floor in the middle of the room was a large star he had marked out with chalk. At each point of the star was a lighted candle and in the middle was a bucket of water. He asked me to strip down to my underwear and step into the middle of the star.

He began chanting unintelligible incantations while picking up each candle in turn and holding it toward the ceiling. After he would chant over each candle, he would allow the wax to drip into the water. When he had done this with all the candles, he proceeded to sprinkle some powdery substance of varying colors into the water, all the while muttering incantations. I was then shown to a dirty little shower stall where I was instructed to bathe with the water from the bucket while he consulted with the spirits to find out what the solution to the problem was.

After my shower, we sat down together and he proceeded to inform me that there was a curse on my life and that angels of death had been assigned to kill me. The only way my death could be averted was if he did some ritual sacrifices to appease the spirits. I would have to provide one white hen, one white goat and some money in order for all this to happen.

Once we embarked on the journey down this road, there was almost no end to all the money and supplies we needed to "appease the gods." Eventually, my mother realized that this man was a charlatan and we stopped our consultations with him. (And judging from the enormity of my deliverance after I became a Christian, the wax bath and farm animals hadn't made a difference.)

This man perfectly fits the definition of a medium: an individual held to be a channel of communication between the earthly world and a world of spirits. As already illustrated, God has strong feelings about mediums and their intervention in the normal course of man's existence. Further demonstration of this fact is in the following verses of scriptures:

> A man or a woman who is a medium, or who has familiar spirits, shall surely be put to death; they shall stone them with stones. Their blood shall be upon them. - Leviticus 20: 27

> When men tell you to consult mediums and spiritists, who whisper and mutter, should not a people inquire of their God? Why consult the dead on behalf of the living? - Isaiah 8:19 (NIV)

Interestingly, the King James Version of the Bible uses the word "wizard" in place of the word "medium." *The Strong's Exhaustive Concordance of the Bible* renders the meaning of the word "wizard" as "a knowing one, a conjurer, by implication, a ghost." The word "wizard" is also translated "magician" or "sorcerer."[5]

Mediums are alive and well in today's society. They are, as evidenced by the advertisement discussed at the beginning of this chapter, slowly but inexorably entrenching themselves into our everyday lives. There is no doubt in my mind that the scheme of Satan is to introduce a counterfeit gospel that supposedly gives man insight into the future and, consequently, the ability to manipulate his own destiny. Man becomes his own god if he controls his own destiny. This is not a new scheme by the enemy. His attack on Eve in the garden of Eden was to convince her that eating of the tree of the knowledge of good and evil would expand her mind and make her like God (Genesis 3:5), thereby giving her the ability to control her own destiny.

The bane of humanity is our desire to be like God, having insight into all things. This is one reason why there is a proliferation of "mind developing" religions that help you evolve from one plane of consciousness to the next, falsely promising greater insight into all things. Hear the distinct warning of the Lord: "Do not turn to mediums or seek out spiritists, for you will be defiled by them. I am the Lord your God" (Leviticus 19: 31 [NIV]).

## Witchcraft

Recently I saw a movie titled "The Craft" to prepare for a teaching I was giving on the occult. The movie was a study in evil. The scenes of levitation, consulting with the dead and with Satan himself were scary enough. Added to the mix were people transforming themselves into other people, creating snakes from thin air and holding séances and rituals to draw on occult powers. And it was all happening among high school girls who were barely past puberty!

Now, I understand that Hollywood is given to sensationalism; after all, that is what sells movies. It cannot, however, be overstated that there are overt elements of real witchcraft that are involved in these types of movies. Among witches that I have talked to, they like to make the distinction between black and white witchcraft. I see it a little more black and white (forgive the pun). It is either God-inspired or demonically inspired. Witchcraft is most definitely not God-inspired, since it sets up other things as gods. Even in Wiccan witchcraft, which supposedly reveres nature, power is seen to come not from a Supreme God but from the wind, air, sea and land (this was actually an integral part of the movie "The Craft," when the main actress sought to consult with dark spirits to ostensibly receive greater power).

*Vines Expository Dictionary of New Testament Words* defines the root word for sorcery and witchcraft as the Greek word *Pharmakia*. It is from this root word that we derive our English word "pharmacy." It primarily signified the use of medicine, drugs, spells; then, poisoning; then, sorcery as used in Galatians 5: 20. It was the use of drugs generally accompanied by incantations and appeals to occult powers, with the provision of various charms, amulets, etc., professedly designed to keep the applicant or patient from the attention and power of demons, but actually to impress the applicant with the mysterious resources and powers of the sorcerer.[6]

In my continuing search for material on the subject of witchcraft, I came across a rather interesting article on the UK News website written by Marcus Tanner. The article is reprinted in its entirety below.

> Football fans in the central African state of Congo were hurling accusations of witchcraft at each other yesterday after a freak blast of lightning struck dead an entire team on the playing field while their opponents were left completely untouched.
>
> The bizarre blow by the weather to all 11 members of the football team was reported in the daily newspaper L'Avenir in Kinshasa, the capital of Congo.
>
> "Lightning killed at a stroke 11 young people aged between 20 and 35 years during a football match," the newspaper reported. It went on to say that 30 other people had received burns at the weekend match, held in the eastern province of Kasai. "The athletes from Basanga (the home team) curiously came out of this catastrophe unscathed."
>
> The suspicion that the black arts might be involved arose firstly because the opposing team emerged unharmed and then again because the score at the time was a delicately balanced one all.
>
> "The exact nature of the lightning has divided the population in this region which is known for its use of fetishes in football," the newspaper commented.
>
> Much of the detail about the match remains obscure as the Congo - officially known as the Democratic Republic of Congo – remains stricken by civil war between the government of Laurent Kabila and rebel forces, backed by

> neighboring Rwanda, in the east of the country.
>
> Witchcraft is often blamed for adverse natural phenomena throughout western and central Africa. It is relatively frequent for football teams to hire witchdoctors to place hexes on their opponents.
>
> In a similar, though less deadly incident in South Africa over the weekend, six players from a local team were hurt when lightning struck the playing field during a thunderstorm.[7]

As a West African, I resent the insinuation that we often blame witchcraft for adverse "natural phenomena" that occur. I know Westerners are skeptical about the occurrences of witchcraft in every day activity, living in such an anaesthetized society. But, come on folks, it doesn't take rocket science to figure out that lightning isn't selective about whom it strikes. It's not as if the men were standing in a straight line or holding hands. In the game of football (soccer in America), people run all over the field. How on earth does lightning selectively identify 11 men from the same team, scattered across the field, and strike them all dead at one time?

Pastor Ted Haggard of New Life Church in Colorado Springs contributed an article in the October 1998 issue of *Charisma* magazine, in which he displayed profound insight into this aspect of witchcraft:

> During the weeks that surround Halloween, people seem to be uniquely aware of the supernatural realm. It is the only holiday in this country that focuses on death and darkness. Halloween is the time when Americans visit haunted houses, hold séances, dress like vampires and warlocks and watch scary movies—all in fun. But many people lack a basic biblical understanding of the spiritual realities associated with death and the devil—and what they don't know can hurt them.[8]

In today's context, witchcraft is more than just witches and warlocks, ghouls and goblins. Satan is wily enough to realize that not everybody is going to buy into the more overt forms of the occult. So, he works through more subtle means, such as rebellion.

On one of King Saul's forays against Israel's archrivals, the Amalekites, God instructed the king not to bring back any spoils of war. This is fairly unusual, as the only way an army could expand their influence and their territorial holdings was by taking spoils of war from their vanquished foes. But God instructed differently this time. However, Saul takes a particular liking to Agag the Amalekite king and decides to spare his life against the command of the Lord. For good measure, the people decide that what is worth doing is worth doing well, and they hold back some of the livestock and cattle.

When the prophet Samuel confronts Saul, he shirks his responsibility and lays the charge squarely at the people's feet.

> Then Samuel went to Saul, and Saul said to him, "Blessed are you of the Lord! I have performed the commandment of the Lord." But Samuel said, "What then is this bleating of the sheep in my ears, and the lowing of the oxen which I hear?" And Saul said, "They have brought them from the Amalekites; for the people spared the best of the sheep and the oxen, to sacrifice to the Lord your God; and the rest we have utterly destroyed." So Samuel said, "Has the Lord as great delight in burnt offerings and sacrifices, as in obeying the voice of the Lord? Behold, to obey is better than sacrifice, and to heed than the fat of rams. For rebellion is as the sin of witchcraft, and stubbornness is as iniquity and idolatry. Because you have rejected the word of the Lord, He has also rejected you from being king."
>
> - I Samuel 15: 13 – 15, 22 – 23

"Rebellion is as the sin of witchcraft." A loaded statement if ever there was one. If this means exactly what it says, then there are quite a few people unaware that they are dealing with spirits of witchcraft. From our high schools to our military branches, from our families to our places of business, people are embracing rebellion. I wonder if they'd act any differently if they knew they were embracing witchcraft, too?

## Necromancy

The two thirteen-year-olds park their bikes under the large oak tree in front of the house and furtively scan the horizon for any signs of adult life. They have been planning this event for two whole weeks. They know that Tommy's mom won't be home today till after 2.00 p.m. Joey nervously clutches a box tightly to his chest. It has cost them all of their allowance from the last two weeks but they are certain that it will be well worth the sacrifice.

They run around the side of the house to the window that Tommy had surreptitiously unlatched that morning before he left for school. They push open the window and gently slide the box with the Ouija Board inside it onto the dining table just inside the window. Carefully, they climb into the house and pull the window shut behind them. What an ingenious plan Joey had come up with, to have their parents sign permission slips allowing them to go on a class field trip. The rest was easy: getting a friend that had dropped out of school to make up fake doctor's appointment slips and then copying their parents' signatures onto the slips.

They have gone to great lengths to ensure that everything goes smoothly as they embark on this adventure of trying to contact Joey's mother, who had been tragically killed in a car wreck a little over a year ago. They have lots of questions to ask her, and all their friends say the best way to contact dead relatives is by using the Ouija Board.

Now the scene is set. With curtains drawn closed, lights turned off and candles glowing eerily, Tommy and Joey are about to take their first unwitting steps into the world of the occult. More specifically, Tommy and Joey are about to delve into the world of necromancy—interaction with the dead to ask questions about the future. (It is also defined as sorcery.)

King Saul lost the throne of Israel because of his dealings with necromancy. In his insecurity and maddened lust for power, Saul chose to violate the principles that God had outlined for Israel to live by. Desperate to know the future because his disobedience had drawn him out of fellowship with God, Saul seeks audience with a medium and tries to find out what the future has in store for him. He did not like what he found out!

Earlier, Saul had put all the mediums and spiritists out of the land because he was committed to trusting in God's ability to deliver and protect Israel. As he begins to fall away from an intimate relationship with God, yielding to disobedience and the cravings of the flesh (a lust for power), he decides to consult a necromancer. His penalty is swift and severe. The very one that he awakens to find out his future from is the one who pronounces judgement and death over him. Samuel declares that Saul and his sons will die at the hands of the Philistines. Soon after, Saul meets his demise.

In this narrative, Saul is a type of our society. Committed to keeping the precepts of their Christian faith alive and well, the pilgrims fled from the tyranny of Great Britain to establish a colony in the Americas that espoused the values that many of them had fought and died for. With the passing of time, these values have come to mean less and less as we have sought for ways to accommodate the values of everyone. In the same manner, Saul abandoned the values that had brought Israel victory over their enemies time and time again, choosing to disobey God. This cost him his kingdom and then his life. What will it cost us?

There is no doubt that necromancy is actively a part of our society today. One of the problems with that is simply the fact that God has clearly spoken against consulting with mediums to revive the spirits of the dead. There is swift reprisal for disobedience to God, as Saul unwittingly discovered. As Solomon wrote, "There is a way that seems right to a man, but its end is the way of death" (Proverbs 14: 12).

The continued acceptance by our society of all forms of behavior, regardless of the moral implications, will surely lead to the eventual destruction of our moral conscience and our desire to submit to the principles of God's word. This will only serve to create anarchy, rebellion and a culture that accepts everything but the truth.

General Douglas MacArthur put it a little more succinctly when he said,

> "In this day of gathering storms, as moral deterioration of political power spreads its growing infection, it is essential that every spiritual force be mobilized to defend and preserve the religious base upon which this nation is founded; for it has been that base which has been the motivating impulse to our moral and national growth. History fails to record a single precedent in which nations subject to moral decay have not passed into political and economic decline. There has been either a spiritual reawakening to overcome the moral lapse, or a progressive deterioration leading to ultimate national disaster."[9]

Neither necromancy nor any other occult practice can give us insight into determining our future. There is only one definite way to ensure that the future will be bright and that we will enjoy good success. Psalms 37:4 states, "Delight yourself also in the Lord, and He shall give you the desires of your heart." If we try to do it any other way, we are just fooling ourselves.

# Media, Mentors, and Memorabilia

## Media

The alarm goes off at 5:00 a.m. sharp. Joe pulls the covers up over his head to shut out the monotonous drone. For the hundredth time he reminds himself that he needs to get a more pleasant-sounding alarm clock. He reaches over in resignation and slams the OFF button.

Immediately, Joe reaches for the TV remote control and turns on the "Today" show. He cranks up the volume so he can hear what's going on above the roar of the shower. After showering and dressing hurriedly, Joe grabs a granola bar and heads out the door.

As the engine of his car roars to life, the radio blares out the latest release from a popular rock group. During the twenty minutes that it takes him to commute to work, Joe switches between channels, frantically trying to locate the most upbeat music he can find to help clear his head from a late night of drinking with the guys. At the office, he grabs a cup of coffee, boots up his computer and logs onto the Internet to check out the stock market quotes. By lunchtime Joe is so wired from sitting in front of the computer that he decides to take a book to the park across the street, sit on a bench and catch up on some reading.

At six-thirty, Joe finally calls it a day and joins the flood of rush hour commuters jockeying for space on the interstate. Thirty minutes later he pulls off the highway into the parking lot of a sports bar and grille where he has arranged to meet with the guys to watch a basketball game and down a few rounds of beer. Around ten o' clock, Joe finally heads home, exhausted from a long, busy day. He settles down in front of the TV and puts on a DVD that he has been meaning to watch. Less than fifteen minutes later Joe falls asleep in front of the TV.

Nearly 18 hours have gone by, and Joe has been inundated with media every single second. Ever had a day like this?

The media's effect is ubiquitous in today's society, encroaching on almost every area of our lives. If left unchecked, the media can become an extremely unhealthy influence on our families, our friends and us. Even if we are very careful about what we watch or listen to, the media can have a subtle but profound impact on our lives.

Consider, for example, a seemingly innocent commercial for the Snickers candy bar. The setting is just outside the gates of heaven. A long line of candidates stand awaiting their interview to see whether or not they'll be allowed into paradise. The candidate that is currently being interviewed is obviously having a difficult time convincing the interviewer of his qualifications for this great celestial reward. He is reminded of his sordid past, including his bachelor's eve party. This is all taking a while, and finally some impatient soul yells out, "Hey, does this line ever move?"

The interviewer, with a look of disgust written across his face, suddenly causes the cloud underneath the impatient soul to suck him right through. "It's moving now!" he remarks smugly. He then glances down at a homely looking middle-aged lady and sneers dryly, "You're a winner." The tag line is, "Not going anywhere soon? Grab a Snickers."

This commercial sets itself up as good, clean fun, but its subtle messages are dangerous. It represents a poor perspective of heaven, God, and the reasons that people go to heaven. It portrays heaven as a place that you earn the right to go to. It suggests that God's angels (or God Himself) are an impatient group of beings just waiting to zap you the minute you step out of line. Finally, the advertisement indicates that you cannot have the assurance of knowing where you will spend eternity until your final demise. According to the Bible, of course, none of these are true.

Now, I'm not necessarily suggesting that the folks who made this commercial are trying to philosophize against an accurate view of heaven. But they are unwittingly influencing people's ideas. The effect of media is so powerful that people's thoughts are impacted whether the media intends to do it or not.

It never ceases to be a source of wonder for me to hear media executives pass off as myth the challenge that violent movies, violent video games, and music have a negative effect on our children. "People make whatever choices they are going to make regardless of the media's influence," they claim. Then they turn around and charge millions of dollars for a sixty-second advertising spot in the middle of the Super Bowl or some other widely viewed event. This just doesn't compute. If, as they claim, the effect that the media has on people's choices were minimal at best, then why would it be a justifiable venture to charge so much money for so little impact?

Many sociologists refer to the under-twenty generation as the MTV Generation. It's a telling title—young people have so imbibed MTV and its popular culture bedfellows that they mirror the characteristics of that world in terms of taste and morals. What would have been considered totally outrageous in the fifties and early sixties would not even warrant the batting of an eyelid among today's generation of young people.

Not so long ago, one of the most popular shows on MTV was a cartoon show titled "Beavis and Butthead." This show propagated everything lewd, crass and debasing. The characters prided themselves on swearing, cursing and performing obscene bodily functions that should only be done in private. Many of their expressions became part of the popular lexicon.

Likewise, Fox TV's ratings have soared because of popular cartoon shows such as “The Simpsons” and “King of the Hill.” The fact that these are cartoon shows in no way reduces the impact of the subtle and overt messages being sent. “The Simpsons” represents everything that is at variance with the teachings of the Bible. The young son, Bart Simpson, addresses his dad, Homer, by his first name, demonstrating his gross disrespect for him. The parents are constantly feuding and speaking disparagingly to one another, even in the presence of their children. Their children hardly get along and are obviously much more intelligent than their parents. To say this is a highly dysfunctional family would be a gross understatement. This, however, is what the media executives see as first rate TV and so they continue to churn it out for higher ratings. As I write this, I am flying at 34,000 feet above the Atlantic in a British Airways Boeing 747-400, and yes, “The Simpsons” is showing.

Sex also sells, and primetime TV parades a lineup of sitcoms that are full of sexual innuendo, both pre-marital and homosexual. Clearly, people have become desensitized to these subtle expressions of rebellion, continually creating the need for more and more stimulation. In its basest form, the influence of various kinds of sexual deviance portrayed by the media in such shows as “Friends” and “Will and Grace” can result in people playing out the physical expressions of their twisted fantasies, as mass murderer Jeffrey Dahmer did a few years ago. By his own admission, Jeffrey’s exposure to pornography stimulated his desire to play out his ultimate sexual fantasy, which involved lying beside an unconscious male while having sex with him. Soon, this alone was not sufficient and he desired to have sexual intercourse with dead bodies (necrophilia). This ultimately led to his killing, dismembering and eating his victims.

Did the media force Jeffrey Dahmer to make the choices he made? Obviously not. It cannot be overstated though, that when a media with so much power is free to call evil good and good evil, people are likely to denigrate to all forms of anti-social behavior.

The media’s influence on our society is irrepressible. This fact was unequivocally driven home to me through the media’s approach to the issue of abortion. In the early years of this debate, much of the media labeled the fundamentalist Christian position “anti-choice,” while the abortion rights advocates were labeled "pro-choice." If anti-choice is the media's preferred term for the opposition to pro-choice, shouldn't the pro-choice movement be referred to as anti-life? Because of this strategic use of vocabulary, Christian fundamentalists who are concerned for women and unborn babies are nearly universally seen as overly negative, narrow-minded bigots.

The Bible has this to say in specific reference to the issue of negative media influences on our hearts and minds:

> My son, give attention to my words; Incline your ears to my sayings.
>
> Do not let them depart from your eyes; Keep them in the midst of your heart;
>
> For they are life to those who find them, and health to all their flesh.
>
> Keep your heart with all diligence, for out of it spring the issues of life. - Proverbs 4: 20 – 23
>
> I will set nothing wicked before my eyes: - Psalm 101: 3a
>
> Then He said to them, "Take heed what you hear." - Mark 4:24a

Why is God so concerned about what we see and hear? Because what we imbibe through our senses has a massive impact on our lives. Just think of the countless cases of anorexia, bulimia and other such terrible spiritual addictions that afflict our society in part because of the media's portrayal of the "ideal" figure for a woman or the consummate body for a man. Low self-esteem has become prevalent in our society because we have allowed the media to define the acceptable standards of beauty. The media must be willing to accept that it plays a vital role in the establishing of popular culture. There is little hope of escaping the influences of all of these interactive media forms unless we define our morality by the absolutes of the Scriptures rather than the dictates of popular culture.

Pornography has ravaged our society in part because of easy access to pornographic websites on the Internet, as well as the proliferation of adult bookstores all advertising their deadly wares. This has destroyed the lives, families and ministries of numerous Christian leaders who have been caught in the web of its enticing allure. My good friend Mike Fehlauer has written an outstanding book titled *Finding Freedom From the Shame of the Past* which deals with the spiritual roots of this area of pornographic media influence, among others, in great detail. It really cannot be overemphasized how important it is for us to protect ourselves and our children from media influences that will ultimately prove destructive to our effective Christian walk.

## Mentors

I recently watched a program on TV about the effects of peer pressure on people's choices. They conducted an experiment with a number of high school young people all together in a room. All the kids except one had been prepped for the experiment by being told to pick the wrong answers to the questions on purpose.

The person conducting the experiment began by showing the teens a number of cards with simple illustrations on them and asking them to match the most identical ones together in pairs. The solutions were fairly obvious. All the kids with the exception of the one who didn't know that it is a staged experiment picked the wrong answers. They then conducted a number of similar experiments with similarly obvious answers. Each time, he was the only one who picked the correct answer. But after this went on for a while, he began to pick the wrong answer intentionally. When asked why he did this, he indicated that since every one else was picking the wrong answers, he didn't want to be the odd one out. He was willing to be consciously wrong about his answers rather than endure the peer pressure of being the only one picking the right answers.

Another interesting story to hit the TV headlines recently is the story of Mary Kay Letourneau, a high school teacher. Mary Kay, who was married with children, did an incomparable job of destroying the values of one of her students, Villi Fulau, who was 14 years old at the time. Mary Kay and Villi became sexually involved with one another until the courts determined that she was in violation of the law because she had molested a minor. She was placed under psychiatric care, told to desist from any further contact with the boy, and given a suspended sentence by the judicial system. Unfortunately, Mary Kay violated all the terms of her suspended sentence by meeting with Villi and carrying on their relationship, of which a baby girl was the result. Mary Kay was promptly placed in prison to carry out an eight-year sentence.

But what makes the story even more intriguing is Mary Kay's family history. Her father had been a powerful and well-connected politician with tremendous political aspirations. He was known as a devout family man who espoused all the values a healthy family man would. But it turned out that he was living a double life and had had affairs with certain female students of his. When it all came to light, his family was devastated and his political hopes were demolished. Mary Kay says that her home was so debilitating to grow up in that she left home and got married to get away from the issues surrounding her family life.

I have stated over and over again that the greatest demons you will fight will be your parents' demons. This is why godly mentors are so valuable in influencing a young person's choices. The only way Mary Kay could have avoided falling into the same pit her father fell into was if she had identified the spiritual strongholds that were over her family and dealt with them early on in her marriage. Even Bill Clinton's choice to have an affair with Monica Lewinsky is a direct reflection of the mentors that existed in his life and the values they taught him about fidelity in marriage.

Unfortunately, negative role models abound today. Howard Stearn, the self-styled "shock jock" of talk show radio, is a classic illustration of this fact. The man is positively neanderthal in his communication skills. It seems that sex, lewd talk and the like are all there is on his mind. But Stearn would do well to remember that his less than positive influence on our youth culture can only serve to further alienate our society from the truth of the Bible. Truth is absolute, and morality will ultimately determine the rise or decline of a society. If people like Howard have anything to do with it, we are on a fast track to social, spiritual, and economic decline

Drew Carey's self-titled sitcom has numerous overt references to sexuality from one show to the next, despite its prime time billing. In spite of its references to sexuality, it commands a whopping $143,000.00

for a thirty-second advertising spot during the show. It cannot be overemphasized that, "garbage in" means "garbage out." These celebrities, regardless of their popularity, wealth or power are not positive role models, neither for our children nor for our society as a whole.

Mentors are life coaches who focus on improving the choices made by the ones into whose lives they are speaking. Make no mistake about it; our friends are also our mentors. Depending on the kind of friends we choose, our mentors can be either positive or negative role models. The Bible speaks clearly to the issue of role models or mentors in our lives.

> "Do not be misled: 'Bad company corrupts good character.'"
> - I Corinthians 15:33 (NIV)

A really poignant reminder for me of the influences of media and mentors in our lives is a commentary by Chuck Colson on his daily radio broadcast, *Breakpoint.* Regarding the Columbine High School shootings in Littleton, Colorado, he said the following:

> It was a test all of us would hope to pass, but none of us really wants to take. A masked gunman points his weapon at a Christian and asks, "Do you believe in God?" She knows that if she says "yes," she'll pay with her life. But unfaithfulness to her Lord is unthinkable. So, with what would be her last words, she calmly answers "yes, I believe in God."
>
> What makes this story remarkable is that the gunman was no communist thug, nor was the martyr a Chinese pastor. As you may have guessed, the event I'm describing took place last Tuesday in Littleton, Colorado. As the Washington Post reported, the two students who shot 13 people, Eric Harris and Dylan Klebold did not choose their victims at random – they were acting out of a kaleidoscope of ugly prejudices. Media coverage has centered on the killers' hostility toward racial minorities and athletes, but there was another group the pair hated every bit as much, if not more: Christians. And there were plenty of them to hate at Columbine High School. According to some accounts eight Christians – four Evangelicals and four Catholics – were killed.
>
> Among them was Cassie Bernall. And it was Cassie who made the dramatic decision I've just described – fitting for a person

whose favorite movie was "Braveheart," in which the hero dies a martyr's death. Cassie was a 17-year-old junior with long blonde hair, hair she wanted to cut off and have made into wigs for cancer patients who had lost their hair through chemotherapy. She was active in her youth group at Westpool's Community Church and was known for carrying a Bible to school. Cassie was in the school library reading her Bible when the two young killers burst in. According to witnesses, one of the killers pointed his gun at Cassie and asked, "do you believe in God?" Cassie paused and then answered, "Yes I believe in God." "Why?" the gunman asked. Cassie did not have a chance to respond; the gunman had already shot her dead.

As her classmate Mickie Cain told Larry King on CNN, "She completely stood up for God. When the killers asked her if there was anyone who had faith in Christ, she spoke up and they shot her for it." Cassie's martyrdom was even more remarkable when you consider that just a few years ago she had dabbled in the occult, including witchcraft. She had embraced the same darkness and nihilism that drove her killers to such despicable acts. But two years ago, Cassie dedicated her life to Christ, and turned her life around. Her friend Craig Moon, called her a "light for Christ." Well, this "light for Christ" became a rare American martyr of the 20th Century.

According to the Boston Globe, on the night of her death, Cassie's brother Chris found a poem Cassie had written just two days prior to her death. It read:

"Now I have given up on everything else

I have found it to be the only way

To really know Christ and to experience

The mighty power that brought

Him back to life again, and to find

Out what it means to suffer and to

Die with Him. So, whatever it takes
I will be one who lives in the fresh
Newness of life of those who are
Alive from the dead."

The best way all of us can honor Cassie's memory is to embrace that same courageous commitment to our faith. For example, we should stand up to our kids when they want to play violent video games. We should be willing to stand up to community ridicule when we oppose access to Internet pornography at the local library.

For the families of these young martyrs, I can only offer deep personal sympathy and the hope that they might take strength from the words Jesus spoke to the woman who honored Him by pouring ointment on His head. "Wherever this gospel is preached in the whole world, what she has done will be told in memory of her" (Matthew 26: 13). "Well done, good and faithful servant. Now enter into the joy of your Lord" (Matthew 25: 23).[1]

(1999 Prison Fellowship Ministries. Reprinted with permission. "Breakpoint with Chuck Colson" is a radio ministry of Prison Fellowship Ministries.)

## Memorabilia

Talking with a pastor friend of mine recently, he related a conversation he had had with some friends of his on the issue of media, mentors and memorabilia. According to him, they easily bought into the idea that media and mentors have a significant impact on our lives, but found it hard to absorb the fact that objects that we bring into our homes can attract demonic activity. But certain types of memorabilia are demonic antennae that can impact a life so dramatically as to change a person's destiny.

King Josiah understood this fact implicitly when he commanded that all the articles from the temple that had been dedicated to Baal and

Asherah were to be burned:

> The king ordered Hilkiah the high priest, the priests next in rank and the doorkeepers to remove from the temple of the Lord all the articles made for Baal and Asherah and all the starry hosts. He burned them outside Jerusalem in the fields of the Kidron Valley and took the ashes to Bethel - II Kings 23:4

In order to restore the presence of God to the temple, King Josiah understood that he needed to cleanse the temple from the negative spiritual input that had infested the sanctuary of the Most High God.

Coming from a Nigerian heritage as I do, this subject is very close to home for me. Before the advent of Christianity in our culture, we were essentially animists, worshipping idols. Different tribes worshipped various gods that supposedly watched over them. They made images of stone, iron and pottery to represent their servitude to these gods. There were effigies made to gods of iron, water, fertility and even to Satan himself. These effigies were brought into the homes of the worshippers as protection over their homes. Some of them even named their children or changed their family names to incorporate the names of these gods in order to demonstrate their devotion and loyalty.

In Nigeria, the god of iron or metal is named Ogun. Devotees of this god took such names as Ogunbiyi, which means, "Ogun gave birth to this one." Sango was recognized as the god of thunder and lightning, and followers took on such names as Sangowawa, meaning, "Sango has come to find (take) this one." My brother-in-law has the ancestral family name of Ogunbanwo, which means "Ogun watch over (protect) this one."

It is a well-known fact that people with ancestral names such as these typically experienced all manner of generational and ancestral bondage. Many of the younger generation in our country who have become Christians are changing their last names and substituting God where the name of the idol used to be. Ogunbiyi is changed to Olubiyi, which means, "This one comes from (or is given) by God." (An interesting side note is that the symbol for the Nigerian Electric Power Authority (NEPA), is a huge statue of the god Sango (pronounced Shaun-go), displayed majestically in front of the enormous sky scraper that houses NEPA on

Lagos Island. Nigeria is known to have a very erratic supply of electricity so that many homes and businesses have their own power generators. The acronym NEPA is commonly referred to as Never Expect Power Always).

This influence of memorabilia has spilled over into various aspects of African culture, but most especially in the arts. Sculptures and paintings depict the people's deep devotion to their gods, and as expatriates flock to different African countries looking for exotic vacations and memorabilia, they end up purchasing spiritual emblems of which they have no understanding and taking them back home as ornaments for coffee tables and mantle pieces. The sad fact is that the spiritual influences that are attached to these "ornaments" are also imported into their homes. An example of this is found in a book that I studied during my university days.

In my art history class we used a book titled *Gardner's Art Through The Ages*. At that time there was not a section in it dedicated exclusively to African art. Imagine my surprise when I recently purchased the tenth edition and found an African art section. Most of the art was of sculptures that I recognized from history and legend as having strong spiritual connotations for the animistic religions of the regions.

My greatest shock, however, was finding a story and a photograph of a priestess's shrine from "Mami Wata" (mother of the sea; also known as mermaid) displayed as art.[2] In the story of Angel's demons in chapter two, I alluded to this spirit when I talked about her having a mansion under the water. Mami Wata worship is not art. It is a well-documented fact in Nigeria that this is a demon-worshipping cult spirit that seeks to seduce and destroy men and make use of their body parts for various fetish rituals.

In Hosea 4:6, God states, "My people are destroyed for lack of knowledge". The ploy of Satan is deception. He will stop at nothing to manipulate truth and circumstances to infiltrate our homes with his demonic hordes through various kinds of memorabilia. On one occasion I took a couple of people from my deliverance team to the home of a precious lady that attends our church in Colorado. She had requested that we come up and pray over her home because she had been incessantly ill.

When we got to her home I sensed an overwhelming presence of death. As we began to pray over the house and cleanse it spiritually, we came across memorabilia of the Egyptian goddess Neferttiti.

Much of Egyptian art is essentially funerary art. The artist was referred to as "He who keeps alive" because life after death was a predominant theme in Egyptian religion and was strongly reflected in their art. The artist's portrayal of a person's image was said to help bring the person back to life after their death. It was thought that the alternate or soul of a person, their "ka," would inhabit the body of the deceased and would continue to live on in an afterlife. This is why Pharaohs were never entombed alone—they were said to require wives and servants in their afterlife. Their servants and wives were typically buried alive with them and so usually died horrifying deaths from asphyxiation..[3]

Little wonder then that a spirit of death had entered this woman's home. Her husband had died prematurely and now we were discerning a spirit of death on her. They had innocently purchased these works of "art" on a vacation to Egypt many years before and placed them in central view in their living room. We explained the spiritual implications of having such articles in her home and she willingly gave them to us to destroy them. We prayed with her and broke the stronghold of the spirit of death over her.

Later that week, she discovered that she had cancer, but it had been discovered in enough time to be treatable. There is little doubt in my mind that the presence of memorabilia from Egypt depicting the likeness of Neferttiti had a lot to do with the presence of the spirit of death that was prevalent in that home.

# Identifying ruling spirits

Over the last decade or so, the Church has become increasingly aware of the realities of spiritual warfare as it relates to different races and people groups and our ability to significantly impact our cities on a spiritual level. While I fully accept that spiritual warfare is largely similar from one race or people group to another, I also believe that there are subtle differences (because of the ancestry and heritage of the different races) that call for unique approaches to this warfare from one race to another. I also believe that demons are concentrated in varying degrees in different areas depending on the lifestyle choices of the people that predominate in that particular area.

Having had the opportunity to travel fairly extensively internationally, I have been able to develop a fascinating perspective on spiritual warfare. I have observed that as a result of the differing spiritual climates from one country or culture to another, there are different ruling spirits that seek to control the lifestyles of the people. As a matter of fact, the recently discovered (at least in its present form) art of spiritual mapping lends credence to this fact.

Spiritual mapping seeks to identify ruling spirits that control different areas of cities as well as measure the effectiveness of targeted prayer.

Spiritual mapping demarcates a city into regions or sections that are identified by certain demographic features. For example, in the city of Colorado Springs, there is a part of town that has a proliferation of liquor stores, low-income housing and a preponderance of drug-related activity. Identifying and mapping these regions serves as an effective tool for intercessors that would like to pray for Colorado Springs in an organized fashion. This system of spiritual mapping also allows churches to track and measure the effectiveness of their prayers that are targeted at a specific area by measuring the changes in crime and drug-related statistics among numerous others. Clearly it is arguable whether the decline of crime or drug use in a particular geographic location is specifically as a result of targeted prayer. If, however, you operate from the biblical premise that indicates that effectual and fervent prayer produces the power to change situations, it is not hard to reconcile the fact of prayer that changes whole cities. The scriptures further appear to confirm this in the following verse:

> For we do not wrestle against flesh and blood, but against principalities, against powers, against the rulers of the darkness of this age, against spiritual hosts of wickedness in the heavenly places. - Ephesians 6:12

Clearly the indication from the above verse suggests that there is indeed a battle in which we are embroiled and that this battle is fought against spiritual forces that are hierarchical. In its original Greek form, the word principalities is translated as a chief or principal ruler; Powers translates as a superhuman force, potentate or jurisdictional authority; rulers of darkness translates as a world ruler of obscurity or shadiness. This in turn comes from a root word that means to seize or retain by use of strength. Interestingly it is highlighted as an epithet of Satan, who seeks to control and dominate people by the use of force. The phrase spiritual hosts of wickedness is a reference to an ethereal, demoniacal spirit of depravity, malice, disease, wickedness, evil and lewdness.

## The backdrop for the battle

Numerous examples exist in scripture where warfare has occurred in the "heavens" between forces of good and evil as the constant battle for the apparent control of humanity is waged. Satan and his minions seek to establish a kingdom that opposes God and all that He represents. God seeks to re-establish the relationship that once existed between Himself and mankind through a relationship with His Son Jesus Christ. This provides the backdrop for the warfare that is continually waged in the spirit realm. In this context it becomes evident that these spiritual battles that are waged in the "heavens" are against ruling spirits that directly influence the lifestyles of cities or regions.

Jesus Himself identified this battle for his disciples in Matthew 24 by highlighting certain signs that He stated would be evidence of the end of the age. Deception, wars, famine, death.

In studying the scriptures further, I believe the reference in Revelation 6:1-8 to be a type (foreshadowing or picture) of the spiritual forces that rule countries, territories and people groups.

> Now I saw when the Lamb opened one of the seals; and I heard one of the four living creatures saying with a voice like thunder, "come and see."
>
> And I looked, and behold, a white horse. He who sat on it had a bow; and a crown was given to him, and he went out conquering and to conquer.
>
> When He opened the second seal, I heard the second living creature saying, "Come and see."
>
> Another horse, fiery red, went out. And it was granted to the one who sat on it to take peace from the earth, and that people should kill one another; and there was given to him a great sword.
>
> When He opened the third seal, I heard the third living creature say, "Come and see." So I looked, and behold, a black horse, and he who sat on it had a pair of scales in his hand.
>
> And I heard a voice in the midst of the four living creatures saying, "A quart of wheat for a denarius, and three quarts of barley for a denarius; and do not harm the oil and the wine."
>
> When He opened the fourth seal, I heard the voice of the fourth

> living creature saying, “Come and see.”
>
> So I looked, and behold, a pale horse. And the name of him who sat on it was Death, and Hades followed with him. And power was given to them over a fourth of the earth, to kill with sword, with hunger, with death, and by the beasts of the earth. - Rev. 6:1 – 8

No doubt the vision of these horses is a representation of the apocalyptic period when the Lamb of God will break the seals on the scrolls that will permit the unleashing of judgment on the earth. However, I believe that they are also a present day spiritual manifestation of spiritual forces that seek to hinder the effective communication of the gospel in our different cities and among the different races.

## The white horse of deception

John the Revelator begins in Rev.6: 2 by identifying the first horse as a white horse upon whom sits a rider that is given a crown.

> And I looked, and behold, a white horse. He who sat on it had a bow; and a crown was given to him, and he went out conquering and to conquer. - Rev. 6:2

It is not unusual for one to assume that this rider is Christ since He appears in His Second Coming riding on a white horse. (Rev. 19:11). This interpretation however, would raise certain problems. The first would be the fact that Christ, during the playing out of this scene is the one in heaven opening the seals. He could not at the same time be the principal figure in the scene unraveling on earth. Second, the last three horses are clearly demonic (war, famine, death) and are released to “hurt” the earth and its inhabitants. (Christ is incapable of evil, as He is the personification of good.) John 10:10 establishes quite clearly that the role of the devil is to kill, steal and destroy while Christ has come to bring abundant life. If this is true, then Christ could not be the rider of the white horse here grouped with this satanic trio. Finally, the devil’s characteristic qualities lend credence to the fact that his purpose for riding out on this white horse would be to conquer nations and people, bringing them under his control. This would support the fact of “wrestling” against spiritual forces that dominate and control lifestyles in whole cities and regions as previously referenced in Ephesians 6:12.

Another passage of reference that could indicate that this white horse and its rider are counterfeits of the Messiah, on a mission to sow deceit and discord is found in 2 Thessalonians.

> Let no one deceive you by any means; for that day will not come unless the falling away comes first, and the man of sin is revealed, the son of perdition, who opposes and exalts himself above all that is called God or that is worshiped, so that he sits as God in the temple of God, showing himself that he is God.
>
> Do you not remember that when I was still with you I told you these things?
>
> And now you know what is restraining, that he may be revealed in his own time.
>
> For the mystery of lawlessness is already at work; only He who now restrains will do so until He is taken out of the way.
>
> And then the lawless one will be revealed, whom the Lord will consume with the breath of His mouth and destroy with the brightness of His coming.
>
> The coming of the lawless one is according to the working of Satan, with all power, signs, and lying wonders, and with all unrighteous deception among those who perish, because they did not receive the love of the truth, that they might be saved.
>
> And for this reason God will send them strong delusion, that they should believe the lie, that they all may be condemned who did not believe the truth but had pleasure in unrighteousness. - 2 Thess. 2:3 - 12

This, according to Rev 6:2, is the mission of the white horse rider: to control the nations through power, signs and lying wonders.

May I suggest that this white horse rider who seeks to imitate the true King is the manifestation of the spirit of deception. He will cause many to herald his coming as Messiah, but he will be the antithesis of good. Unfortunately, according to the preceding scripture, there are many that will buy into the lies and deception that he brings. Also, in Paul's first letter to Timothy he says;

> Now the Spirit expressly says that in latter times some will depart from the faith, giving heed to deceiving spirits and doctrines of demons... - 1Tim. 4:1

This spirit of deception has already begun to do its deadly work in the Church today in greater dimension than ever before.

Another natural consequence of this quest for "success" is the break down of the family. As men sought to become wealthy by any means, many of them turned to drug dealing, which was thought to provide a handsome and quick return financially. Others turned to armed robbery and other such fraudulent practices, also hoping to reap a large return. Inevitably many of them ended up in prison. The idea that the use of drugs, indiscriminate sex and other such pursuits will provide happiness and fulfillment has turned out to be a satanic ruse designed to draw people away from a committed relationship with the Lord. Unfortunately many that have walked this road have found nothing but emptiness at its end. Ask Bill Clinton. Ask O.J. Simpson. Clearly the Spirit of God has outlined this for us in the following passage:

> There is a way that seems right to a man, but its end is the way of death. - Proverbs. 14:12

We must re-focus our attention on the realities of Kingdom living. Jesus Christ is Lord regardless of the circumstance. In order to live victorious and fulfilled lives we must place our trust in His unchanging Word in our ever-changing world. The ultimate deception is in the lie that we can find fulfillment, peace and happiness in anything other than an intimate relationship with Jesus Christ.

## The red horse of war

The second horse that rides out is a red horse and it symbolizes war and wanton destruction.

> Another horse, fiery red, went out. And it was granted to the

> one who sat on it to take peace from the earth, and that people should kill one another; and there was given to him a great sword. - Rev. 6:4

This horse and its rider are commissioned to take peace from the earth and wreak havoc among the nations. This is a picture of war and strife. The fallouts of war are almost innumerable. Fear motivates people to do the unthinkable. In war, fear becomes a dominant spiritual force. People are uncertain of their survival. Consequently, people denigrate to sub-human levels, fighting for their very survival. Looting and even killing is not uncommon, as people will do anything just to get food, water or a place to shelter. The Watts riots of Los Angeles a few years ago precipitated by the Rodney King beating are an excellent representation of this fact. These circumstances tend to create dehumanizing conditions. These conditions further serve as a distraction from daily living and the successful completion of set tasks and goals. There is a spiritual context in which this becomes applicable to the Church.

War is symbolic of strife and disunity and the Bible states:

> For where envy and self-seeking (strife - KJV) exist, confusion and every evil thing are there. - James 3:16

And also:

> … If a house is divided against itself, (disunity) that house cannot stand. - Mark 3:25

Strife, disorder and disunity are manifest in numerous ways from one social group or society to another. In the context of our culture, these differences range from racial to religious convictions even among those who claim to be Christians. This produces effects similar to those that are produced wherever there is war. These conditions are often reflected in communities that are lacking in social and moral order.

My country of birth, Nigeria, serves as a perfect model attesting to this fact. Tribalism and religious contention, among others, have created instability and anarchy. In our recent past, we have had to contend with numerous changes in government because of military coups and rampant corruption and mismanagement of the countries resources. Like a country at war, social and moral disorder have become systemic and characterize the order of the day.

In many communities globally, the devil has enabled broken marriages, alcoholic/abusive parents, loose morality, low self-esteem, sibling rivalry, Aids and other STD's among numerous other destructive behavioral patterns. These conditions force young men and women to turn to avenues that they believe will provide solace and comfort. The inevitable consequence is drug abuse, multiple sexual partners, gang banging and other expressions of violence and abuse. These in turn lead to high mortality rates and an absence of peace and stability. It must be identified for what it is, a spirit of war that ultimately seeks to destroy and kill. Here in the USA, the incidences of kids killing kids in schools have left sociologists baffled. The only pattern that consistently seems to emerge across the board is that all the kids involved in the incidences were socially and morally dissatisfied.

It is only when this spirit is identified that we are able to destroy it and break its stronghold over our communities. The manifestations of this spirit that are so rampant in our communities are not just a socio-economic problem that is addressed by the welfare system. It is fairly evident that none of the numerous social programs have even made a dent in this growing spiritual problem. However in communities where the church is recognizing the spiritual root of this problem and addressing it with spiritual warfare, as well as an open display of God's love, it is clear to see that in-roads are being made. The absolutely incredible programs being run by Tommy Barnett and Jim Bakker in Phoenix and Los Angeles are examples of what transformation can occur in the inner cities where the drug culture is so prevalent.

It is therefore of vital importance to the proper evolution of our culture that we address spiritual problems with spiritual solutions. Intercession, spiritual warfare, the breaking of generational curses, deliverance as well as the proper re-education (through the Scriptures) of our communities is essential if we must destroy this spiritual stronghold.

The sense in which the drug culture, the absence of fathers in the homes, alcoholism and various other social ills relate to war and strife is evidenced by the fact that all of these detract from focusing on the task at hand. The inability to live a purposeful life creates a lack of appreciation for living. This in turn produces a lack of desire to invest in anything of lasting value and consequently creates an absence of any kind of value system that will produce a fruitful life.

## The black horse of famine

As earlier stated, war distracts you from the task at hand. With our focus directed at conflict, there is usually the consequence of famine, as people are too busy warring to find time to concentrate on planting and harvesting food, necessary for their very survival.

The third horse that rides out is a black horse. This horse represents famine. A natural consequence of war, this spirit (famine) seeks to destroy the very fabric of society by creating inhumane conditions of living.

> When He opened the third seal, I heard the third living creature say, "Come and see." So I looked, and behold, a black horse, and he who sat on it had a pair of scales in his hand.
>
> And I heard a voice in the midst of the four living creatures saying, "A quart of wheat for a denarius, and three quarts of barley for a denarius; and do not harm the oil and the wine." -- Rev. 6: 5– 6

There are a couple of ways in which famine as a driving spiritual force becomes a hindrance to the ability of the average person to receive the gospel. The living conditions and environment in the ghettos and poorer, predominantly minority neighborhoods do not provide for adequate hygiene or healthy eating habits. This is primarily because of the lack of education and resources to provide decent infrastructure to support these communities. Interwoven with this spirit of famine is a spirit of poverty. Famine has manifested itself as poverty in the poorer, less affluent communities where people have learned to survive on whatever is available because they do not have the means to provide themselves a healthier diet. They also lack the proper education to afford them the opportunity to provide a better standard of living.

Consequently, there is resignation to what they consider to be an inescapable plight. This can lead to alcoholism and drug addiction as a means of escaping the harsh realities of their environment. When this mindset takes root in certain communities, people become insular and life loses its value. This subtle scheme of Satan is designed to keep people conditioned to believing that they have been abandoned and forsaken by a God who claims to be love personified. If their poverty-ridden and malnourished lives are evidence of a loving God, then are they not better off without Him?, they ask. This satanic web of lies has been woven so deeply into the fabric of present-day post-Christian American culture, that many communities believe that the only recourse they have to ensure their continued survival is to pursue any means available (good or bad), that provides some semblance of respite from their hardship, no matter how temporary.

This is not an unlikely strategy of Satan as his ploy is to keep people bound in such abject poverty as to cause them to become morally bankrupt. The connection here is the fact that one who is morally bankrupt is ill-equipped to recognize that the battle for survival is as much a spiritual battle as it is an economic one. One who does not see the enemy against which they are fighting, is often unable to articulate a proper strategy to defeat this foe. The word of God holds little value under these circumstances in waging an effective campaign against Satan. The focus on physical survival distracts you from the more relevant task of spiritual survival which itself produces insight for physical survival. This is not unlike the picture painted earlier of war as a catalyst to famine. Just as war distracts you from the business of everyday living, so the relentless struggle for physical survival distracts you from the more necessary pursuit of spiritual survival. This is one of the more subtle schemes of Satan to keep the young, struggling person from the active pursuit of God.

The Bible paints a clear picture for us in this regard:

> "Therefore do not worry, saying, 'What shall we eat?' or 'What shall we drink?' or 'What shall we wear?' For after all these things the gentiles seek. For your heavenly Father knows that you need all these things. But seek first the kingdom of God and His righteousness, and all these things shall be added to you." - Matt. 6: 31-33

The primary focus of the above verses is not the fact that people are seeking after material provision, but more the fact that seeking after a relationship with God is the avenue to providing a godly lifestyle attendant with the necessary material blessings.

The second way in which famine becomes a hindrance to people's ability to receive the gospel, lies in the fact that these impoverished communities begin to take on a sense of victimization. They see themselves as the unfair victims of the lowest socio-economic class of a society that is somewhat intolerant of the less fortunate. This in turn causes these communities to become distrusting of the existing civil authority structure and inter-dependent on themselves. The reason for this is because they believe that no one else is interested in their advancement outside of their own communities.

The lack of exposure to any other form of community living beyond that in which they have been raised, breeds fear. People tend to fear what they do not understand. From their perspective, the system is designed to work against them to keep them from ever succeeding. The issues then become larger than just poverty but take on a whole new dimension that includes racial tension. The Old Testament Prophet, Amos states his case as follows:

> "Behold, the days are coming," Says the Lord God, "That I will send a famine on the land, not a famine of bread, nor a thirst for water, But of hearing the words of the Lord. They shall wander from sea to sea, and from north to east; They shall run to and fro, seeking the word of the Lord, but shall not find it. In that day the fair virgins and strong young men shall faint from thirst." - Amos 8: 11-13

If Amos were alive today witnessing the problems of this generation, he would probably see a clear picture of these verses in a large number of our communities. The Psalms state that God resides in "Mount Zion on the sides of the North" (Psalm 48: 2 NKJV), but people are running from the north to the east seeking after the word of the Lord. Obviously they will not find it there, just like the African-American will not find the solution to his problems in African religions. This famine is spiritual and can only be satiated by establishing a meaningful relationship with the Lord Jesus Christ.

## The pale horse of death

The ultimate purpose of Satan according to John 10: 10 is to steal, to kill and to destroy. He will stop at nothing to ensure that this process is carried out consistently albeit succinctly.

The fourth and final horse that rides out is a pale (mangy) horse of death.

> So I looked, and behold, a pale horse. And the name of him who sat on it was Death, and Hades (Hell) followed with him. And power was given to them over a fourth of the earth, to kill with sword, with hunger, with death, and by the beasts of the earth. - Rev. 6:8

If there was ever any doubt as to the truly demonic origin of these horsemen, it is certainly laid to rest in this verse as the scripture makes abundantly clear what evil intentions they have. Death, the bible says, is the final foe that shall be defeated (I Cor. 15: 26). This is a last ditch effort by Satan to rally his troops for a final foray against the Kingdom of God. The Bible is explicitly clear about the fact that this effort is an exercise in futility. Satan and his demonic hordes are soundly defeated.

> "O Death, where is your sting? O Hades (Hell), where is your victory?" - I Cor. 15: 55

This truth must penetrate the hearts and minds of our communities. The ploy of Satan here is to convince the less fortunate that their economic, social and spiritual plight is beyond salvage. Nothing is further from the truth. The reason Jesus died on the cross for the sins of mankind was, and indeed still is, the redemption of mankind from every plight that has befallen him, and by so doing, to reconcile him with his creator. This horseman works hand in hand with deception, war (strife), and famine to ensure that the average person views his situation as helpless and hopeless. If this spirit successfully takes hold of our communities, inevitably both physical and spiritual death are the consequences of that stronghold.

Fervent prayer and intercession must be made on behalf of our communities (particularly for the younger generation), to re-orient their focus on Jesus Christ and His completed work at Calvary. These demonic strongholds must be utterly destroyed to enable them break free from the mindsets of racial inequality, a lack of identity, poverty and numerous other destructive social patterns. It is however, only after the enemy has been properly identified that the proper weapons can be employed to defeat that enemy. We are committed to the battle knowing that the victory is already assured. It is my sincere and fervent prayer, that this revelation of the spiritual strongholds we are up against, will enable us fight the battle more precisely. Remembering always that,

> ...The weapons of our warfare are not carnal but mighty in God for pulling down strongholds, Casting down arguments and every high thing that exalts itself against the knowledge of God, bringing every thought into captivity to the obedience of Christ, And being ready to punish all disobedience when your obedience is fulfilled. - II Cor. 10: 4-6

# The Role of Deliverance in Church Growth

## New England renewed

In March of 2000, I accepted an invitation to minister at New Life Christian Fellowship in Biddeford, ME, where my good friend Jeff Tarbox is Senior Pastor. At the time, I did not know Jeff and I accepted the invitation primarily because I sensed God wanted me to go there. The invitation was to conduct a four-day deliverance seminar for the 800-member church. Jeff was by no means a novice in the area of deliverance, but felt that he needed a strong outside voice to add credibility and legitimacy to what he had begun.

Right away, people around me questioned whether I ought to be going on this trip. They said that New England was a spiritually destitute area and that I might be wasting my time. In obedience to God, I went anyway.

It was an unbelievable four days of ministry. People were set free. Generational curses were broken. We systematically explored all the issues of deliverance surrounding a local church and how the breaking of spiritual bondage ultimately leads to supernatural growth in the church. I prophesied by the Spirit of God that as the church continued to walk in its newfound revelation of deliverance and emotional healing, they would experience exceptional growth and double within a year's time.

In March of 2001, I went back to do a conference titled "Igniting the Flame in New England," focusing on city strategies through deliverance and spiritual warfare. The church had more than doubled in size! Testimonies continue to pour out on a regular basis, and the church has continued to develop a heightened awareness of prayer and deliverance. After a long dry spell, ministry is exciting again, and other ministers are clamoring to go and visit an area that they previously considered spiritually dead.

Another New England church I ministered deliverance at, The Lord's Gathering Church, has birthed another church and taken spiritual oversight of yet another, creating a strong network of three churches. They are growing in leaps and bounds. The pastor, Ron Satrape, recently called me bubbling with excitement to report that they had finished the year in the black financially for the first time in their history.

Those of us ministering to and/or living in the New England area have a new confidence. We have no doubt that New England will soon capture the spiritual attention of America once again—just as it did in the days of George Whitefield at the advent of the Great Awakening of the 1700's.

You see, deliverance is essential to church growth. Deliverance brings tremendous healing to individuals, which enables them to see the power of God at work in a tangible way in their lives. In turn, the local church is empowered to release the people into their different callings with strength and maturity. Thus, more and more people can share the burden of ministry, enabling the Body of Christ to spread like wildfire.

This is what I do. I have a heart for the local church and served as an assistant local church pastor at New Life Church in Colorado Springs for many years. I also have a heart for seeing people set free from demonic bondage. I believe that deliverance and local church ministry (and, therefore, city transformation) are intrinsically connected. They cannot be separated. Dr. C. Peter Wagner tells me that I might be the only person that he is aware of that travels around the world teaching deliverance and setting up teams in the local church with a view to church growth and city transformations. I do not know if I am the only one teaching this message, but I do know that I have seen supernatural transformations occur both in individual lives and on a corporate level in churches as a result of this type of ministry.

## Revival or Reformation?

Since I am not providing a theological treatise of accurate or acceptable definitions of contemporary Christian terms, I will take the liberty to define revival the way I've heard it defined by the average Joe, sitting in the average pew, in your average church, on any given Sunday.

Revival from Joe's perspective is essentially a sustained visitation of the manifest presence of the Holy Spirit. In other words, good stuff happening because God is noticeably present. This visitation can take on a variety of forms but ultimately serves to turn believers' focus back to God and renew in them a sense of awe and reverence for the holiness, majesty and life-giving power of the Holy Spirit.

While revival by this definition is good and certainly necessary to sustain an awareness of the holiness of God in the church, its effect holds little interest for people who aren't already in church. What they need is not revival, but reformation.

In the chapter on the role of deliverance in city transformation, I tell the stories of four cities that were transformed through reformation in the churches. The intriguing thing about each one of the stories is that the transformations only came after sustained spiritual warfare and deliverance in the local churches. By definition, "transformation" or "reformation" suggest a complete change. This is what we need in our churches. With all due respect to revival specialists, we need more than just a sustained visitation of the Holy Spirit. We need Him to take up permanent residence in our churches so that He maintains full control of all that we do.

The problem with "revival" is that it always draws attention to the one through whom the move of God comes. When transformation or reformation happens, it bypasses human vessels and points all eyes towards God. When you read the story of the transformation of the town of Almolonga, Guatemala (in chapter 9) you cannot help but see the power of God at work, and you are left thinking of Him, not the people who served there. And even though lives were lost in the spiritual battle for the reformation of Cali, Colombia, attention is drawn not to the ones who died, but to the power of the Holy Spirit.

In short, the Body of Christ needs to focus. The move of God that ultimately brings transformation does not always look attractive. Jesus healed a blind man with a mudpack made of spittle, an act that defied the sensibilities of the Pharisees and offended their notions of cleanliness. Why did Jesus do it that way when he could have just as easily touched the man's eyes with clean hands? Because he was making a point—it's God's power that matters, not our expectations of how that power should come.

We don't need to sensationalize the gospel or make it palatable according to the dictates of our culture. All we need to do is present the truth in love and a demonstration of power. Paul, writing to the church in Corinth said,

> And I, brethren, when I came to you, did not come with excellence of speech or of wisdom declaring to you the testimony of God. For I determined not to know anything among you except Jesus Christ and Him crucified. I was with you in weakness, in fear, and in much trembling. ***And my speech and my preaching were not with persuasive words of human wisdom, but in demonstration of the Spirit and of power***, that your faith should not be in the wisdom of men but in the power of God.
>
> - 1 Corinthians 2: 1 – 5, emphasis mine

A few years back I had the opportunity to minister at a church in Florida for a three-day deliverance seminar that addressed how deliverance relates to local church growth. People were set free from things that had plagued them for years. I specifically recall one lady who had been sexually molested as a child. She was a key intercessor for the ministry and loved the Lord desperately. Unfortunately, she had lived for years under the misconception that God did not and could not love her. She was convinced that the abuse was her fault. Somehow, she reasoned, she must have done something to encourage it. This had grievously affected her relationship with her husband and she was unable to enjoy intimacy with him. Her deliverance brought tremendous growth for her family and shortly thereafter she and her husband began to lead the marriage ministry in the church.

There's no way to rationally qualify how powerful the effect of deliverance can be on a local church. Deliverance affects the very core of people's lives. The Florida church had assumed for years that all was well with this lady. Her freedom released a new understanding of the love of God upon the entire church. If she could still be set free, maybe I can, too!

People are attracted to strength, compassion and truth. All of these ingredients are present in a church that has gone through deliverance and seen the power of God break all sorts of bondage off their lives. The truth is that deliverance in the local church brings more than just individual freedom. It builds tremendous faith in the efficacy of the Word of God—not only in the lives of the ones experiencing it, but also in the lives of the ones witnessing it.

Consider the following testimonies from various churches where I have had the opportunity to conduct deliverance seminars and train leaders for deliverance ministry in their local assemblies. (Note: Sola is my lovely wife!)

*Dear Joseph and Sola,*

*I can't begin to thank you enough for bringing Yeshua Ministries to NC3. Our church has definitely been blessed by your visit and teachings. The testimonies of the people are continuing to filter in. They are full of praise, amazement, and awe at what God has accomplished and continues to accomplish in their lives. I am so grateful for all you have done for our flock. I look forward to continuing the process that was begun that weekend...*

*Denver, Colorado*

*Dear Pastor Thompson,*

*Greetings in the name of our Lord and Savior Jesus Christ... The first time you entered the room to teach and minister to us on "Demons and Deliverance," I knew God was going to speak to me through you...God said to me, "Andrew, you need to attend the Deliverance ministry training." I knew God wanted to speak to me specifically, because my attending would mean I would have to sacrifice those work days (I own and manage a vegetarian food business)... Pastor Thompson, I just wish to express my sincere thanks for your impartation into the church (ATC) and into me personally. We will never be the same again...*

*ATC, Barbados*

*Hi Karen**

*I haven't written in a while and thought you might like an update. God is still working around this place and we are all excited!*

*...There is continuing evidence of deliverance from bondages from your visit. Last night at cell group, Jill mentioned that she hasn't been afraid when Kenny is gone since she was delivered from fear at the conference. And Julie is such a blessing! She has become so much more comfortable in the role of pastor's wife. I'm just so encouraged to see so much more freedom in us all, and be a part of what God is doing in this area! Not us, but God!! God is just MUCH MORE! I love you all, and continue to pray His blessings on you!*

*Sayre, OK*

**(Karen is one of the deliverance team ministers that travel with me)*

*Dear Rev. Thompson,*

*I have been meaning to write you this letter for the last 3½ years now and have never been able to do so due to my emotions and when you read on you will understand why.*

*In October of 1998, my parents came to visit with me. They attended worship at Springs Community and you happened to have been preaching that weekend. Growing up in an Eastern Orthodox religion that is very legalistic and formal and hate to admit, very, very boring for me. It was such a breath of fresh air to hear my father say, "I liked that guy, I really enjoyed the sermon."*

*...From that moment on, my father always recalled that experience and always brought up the fact how nice you were, what a good job you did and how much he enjoyed the service... Well, this March 13th will be 3 years since my father passed away and he died from cancer, something we never expected in a million years. The cancer just ate him alive. It was a hard 3 months, my traveling back and forth each weekend to Chicago to spend time with Dad, always wondering if that would be the last time I would see him alive.*

*During my visits, my dad often asked of you and always recalled that evening and had asked if I had seen you or had you been back at our church...My parents were believers, my dad loved the book of Job and he would have us read Job and Psalms to him and during those readings if he were able to talk, he would often mention you.*

*I know that my father is with our Almighty Father in heaven. I miss my dad, but am truly happy that he is where he is.*

*I just want you to know what an impact you made on my dad. You only shook his hand and were briefly introduced; nonetheless you were brought up so many times during his illness. I just wonder how many seeds you indirectly helped plant through my dad. So I am keeping my promise and want you to know how much I appreciate you and your ministry. We are so pleased that you have become friends with our Pastor Steve and have become a good friend to our church. I so enjoy and look forward to your visit. I always tell Pastor Steve and Pastor Ron to go out of town so you can come back to us.*

*Olivia, Colorado Springs, CO*

*Dear Friends,*

*Just so you know who is sending this letter, your group stayed at our daughter and son-in-law's house during the conference. How can we ever thank your group enough? How can we ever thank Jesus enough for using you as his vessels to free those once captured with burdens and bondage? It would take at least a hundred pages to tell you what has happened to us after that incredible weekend.*

*I will just touch on some highlights for me. The best way to explain it is, the Holy Spirit was renting and now He has a home in us. He has opened our eyes and ears, we are seeing and hearing things from the Holy Spirit like never before. The romance is back in our marriage, I feel fifteen years younger; my wife has taken on a glow that is from God and God alone. [Joseph's notes: One of the members of my deliverance team often calls deliverance a "spiritual face lift" as it appears to take years off your countenance after you've been set free.]*

*I went to a prayer meeting and the man who said the following had no idea that my wife and I had attended the deliverance conference. I will try and quote what he said to the best of my recollection, "Richie, will you tell your wife how great she looked Sunday at church." Then he shook his head and said, "There is something different about her, something has changed."*

*To me the whole deliverance conference was a blur. To be honest, I didn't think anything had happened. Was I wrong! My wife extends her heartfelt thanks to the ladies on the deliverance team for their deep discerning. What words are adequate enough to say to your whole team except, "Thank you, thank you in the name of our wonderful Lord Jesus Christ."*

*Portsmouth, New Hampshire*

## Grow a mega-church? Me?

Clearly the introduction of deliverance and spiritual warfare into a local church strengthens the local assembly and in time produces conversion growth in the church. Sustained conversion growth ultimately leads to mega-churches. The preceding testimonies are witness to the fact that, as churches become spiritually healthier through deliverance, the people are more inclined to share the gospel with friends and relatives that are not saved. In that context, deliverance becomes less ethereal and more a part of dealing with everyday life issues.

Should we all aspire to grow mega churches? Is the primary reason for deliverance in the local church so that we can expand our churches numerically? I believe that the simple answer to this often-controversial question is, resoundingly, "Yes!" Obviously there are certain other factors to be considered in the numerical strength of a church, such as city demographics, population, location of a church, accessibility, etc. But at the end of the day, church is about people. The reason we do church is to positively impact our communities by coaching people in the various issues of everyday godly living. If churches in a city are doing this the right way, then all the churches should be experiencing conversion growth, which translates into mega-churches.

Though we don't often think of it this way, deliverance is a rudimentary key to ensuring that the saints are brought to maturity. It is an essential part of local church ministry.

# The Role of Deliverance in City Transformation

It's late in the evening and the lights are out in most of the homes on Capital Boulevard. Except for a few vagrants foraging through the garbage for scraps of food, the streets are devoid of life. A deafening silence hangs over the little town of Asgard as ominous storm clouds gather, casting eerie shadows against the backdrop of gray buildings.

A few of the more confident townsfolk tentatively peek through their shutters, but most of the inhabitants huddle together in their living rooms, whispering, waiting, wondering. The mysterious and gory deaths of four of the townsfolk at last year's celebration of the feast have left a bitter taste in their mouths, and they can't help but wonder what this year's celebration has in store for their close knit community.

It is the feast of All Hallows. Unseen to the natural eye, there is a flurry of activity in the town of Asgard. This is the one feast that the demons look forward to, the one celebration all year that pays homage to ghouls, goblins and ghosts, darkness and evil. It is the time of year when the line between the dark spirit world and the human world is thinnest. The demons swarm in like hungry locusts looking to devour everything in their path. But they are not here as uninvited guests. You see, unwittingly, the inhabitants of Asgard have invited them into their town, homes and lives.

Sound like another Frank Peretti bestseller? Unfortunately, this is not fiction. Like Peretti's books, the town above is fictional, but unlike his books, the story line is real.

## Open doors lead to open hearts

The Bible is full of warnings against opening ourselves up to the spirit world of darkness, and reminds us that we are continually in a battle that is not being waged against humans but against unseen spiritual forces in the heavenly places. One of many doors that open our cities up to the dark world of the occult is the celebration of Halloween. Among numerous other practices that are an inadvertent venture into the occult, the celebration of this feast leaves us exposed to the influx of the demonic.

Halloween is a feast that celebrates the dead and the dark spirit world. As unsuspecting, well-meaning people delve into all sorts of "fun" things like "trick or treat" and dressing up in costumes (the more fiendish or devilish the better), they open themselves up to spiritual influences that they may not even be aware of.

The origin of Halloween should serve as a warning for us to stay away from such activities. The celebration of Halloween dates back to the ancient Celtic people. They lived about 2000 years ago in the geographic area that today marks out Ireland, the United Kingdom and France. The feast, originally known as the feast of Samhain (pronounced sow-ain), was celebrated on November 1 in commemoration of their New Year. The Celts believed that on the night before the New Year, the boundary between the world of the living and the world of the dead became blurred. On October 31, the eve of the feast, they believed that Samhain, who was generally recognized as the lord of death, assembled the spirits of all who had died during the previous year. During this time, it was said that the spirits of the dead returned to earth to visit the living.

During the actual celebration of the feast, crops and animals were burned on a huge bonfire as sacrifices to appease the appetite of Samhain. By the 800's the influence of Christianity had spread into Celtic lands, and in the seventh century, Pope Boniface IV designated November 1 All Saints' Day to honor saints and martyrs. This celebration was also called All-hallows or All-hallowmas (from Middle English Alholowmesse meaning All Saints' Day) and the night before it, the night of Samhain, began to be called All-hallows Eve and, eventually, Halloween.[1]

It must be understood that no matter how much we disguise it, in its modern day application, the celebration of Halloween cannot be divorced from the accompanying spiritual implications and the attendant demonic attachments. This opens the spiritual door that gives those spirits of death and witchcraft free reign in our neighborhoods and cities. By the same token, various other unwitting forays into the dark spiritual world no less result in an influx of the controlling spirits that empower that lifestyle choice.

## Recognizing spiritual climates

There are certain spiritual climates that are particularly conducive to the work of demons. This serves to strengthen the notion that demons are not evenly distributed among the human race. For example, the lifestyle choices in the city of San Francisco make it more conducive to demons that actively influence the homosexual lifestyle. Spirits that control and influence witchcraft are certainly more comfortable in Salem, Massachusetts than they would be in, say, Colorado Springs, Colorado. This means that the battle for control of our cities' spiritual climates must be fought on a spiritual level. In Ephesians 6, we are told that we wrestle not against flesh and blood, but against principalities, powers, wicked spirits in the heavens and the rulers of the darkness of this world. No doubt, we are embroiled in a bitter struggle for supremacy in which our enemies are unseen. The prize? The souls of humanity.

The battle for gaining spiritual control of our cities is not only essential, but also primary. You see, our call as the Church is to reach those that are on the outside of a personal relationship with Jesus. The premise for this battle is the fact that Jesus said He came to seek and save those who are lost. To this end He has commissioned us to be players in this continually unraveling plan of salvation. Satan on the other hand, is committed to ensuring that the plan of God does not come to pass. As we established in chapter three, this is his primary purpose.

Not long ago, I sat down with Dr. C. Peter Wagner to discuss specifics about this book and about deliverance in general. I came out of that meeting with a renewed sense as to the profound role of deliverance in city transformation and church growth. You see, Peter has been a professor of church growth for more than thirty years at the renowned Fuller Theological Seminary. He recently "retired" to establish the Wagner Leadership Institute, which provides training for those already involved in Christian ministry in one form or another. One of the things that was highlighted in my mind at that meeting was Peter's decision to downscale the focus and emphasis of his ministry to include the Apostolic, Prophetic, Prayer and Deliverance ministries. At more than seventy years of age, Peter has reached a stage in his ministry and calling where he sees the need to distill the vital from the mundane. Clearly these areas of ministry upon which he has chosen to focus are not only relevant to the Church today, but also extremely vital for the continued effectiveness of the New Apostolic churches.

In his book, *Churchquake*, Peter defines the New Apostolic Churches as a reformation that is an "extraordinary work of God at the close of the twentieth century which is to a significant extent changing the shape of Protestant Christianity around the world." This reformation is significantly impacting the way we look at global evangelization and intercession.[2]

In identifying churches of the New Apostolic Reformation, it is clear that there are certain common denominators in their approach to ministry. One of those common denominators is the recognition of the need for spiritual mapping. (See chapter 6 for a definition of spiritual mapping.) Because these churches recognize the need to become significant and relevant in their cities, they also recognize the need to identify the various spiritual strongholds that rule in the different regions of their cities. The establishing of the World Prayer Center in Colorado Springs, Colorado is a step towards recognizing this need for more targeted and coordinated efforts towards city transformation.

## The battle strategy

Ted Haggard is the Senior Pastor of New Life Church in Colorado Springs, where I served as Associate Pastor for over four years. Ted often tells the story of his call to start a new church in the city. About 16 years ago, Ted and his wife, Gayle, moved to Colorado Springs to begin a church in the basement of their home in response to God's instructions to Ted. Recognizing that the city had no significantly large churches and that new age philosophies and witchcraft seemed to be the dominant religions, Ted embarked on a series of prayer walks all over the city. He would check into a hotel for three days and walk around that particular area praying for the inhabitants that lived in that part of the city as well as identifying and pulling down spiritual strongholds that appeared to dominate that area. To the natural eye, nothing significant was happening, but in the spirit realm, pressure was being brought to bear on the forces of darkness that had ruled the region without opposition for so long.

Proof that Ted's persistent prayer was beginning to make a significant impact was the fact that the witches were up in arms and began to openly place sacrificial objects like dead animals, feathers and the like in bowls all around his property. The local church pastors began to meet for prayer frequently and took it upon themselves to begin to intercede for the salvation of the entire city. (The Bible indicates that the local church pastors are the gatekeepers to the city (i.e. spiritual watchmen) and have the responsibility to cover the city in prayer.) The long-term effects of these prayers are that Colorado Springs, a city of half a million people, has more than twelve mega-churches (over 1500 attendees). Also, the local police department noticed that areas where Christians had walked in prayer recorded significantly lower incidences of crime. They began to contact the network of churches every time they encountered an area of increased criminal activity, requesting that the area be saturated with prayer and prayer walking.

This is not exclusive to Colorado Springs. Cities all over the United

States as well as in other nations are experiencing a similar response to prayer and spiritual warfare.

A few years ago, shortly after I went on staff at New Life, a reporter from National Public Radio (NPR) in Chicago came to Colorado Springs to do a story on prayer walking. She was completely fascinated by the idea that people would go around praying for people they did not know with no more motivation than to bless them. I was assigned the task of setting up interviews for her, so we were able to spend ample time talking. She kept inquiring whether we solicited donations in the course of prayer walking. I informed her that we didn't even come in direct contact with those we were praying for and that they probably were not even aware that we were praying for them. I further explained that the idea behind prayer walking was not entirely different from an army engaging in warfare. "In fact," I told her, "prayer walking is spiritual warfare." We engage the enemy in battle, using prayer and deliverance as our spiritual weaponry, beating back the forces of darkness.

This reporter's stated objective was to bridge the gap between the secular and the religious by doing a story that highlighted the common ground between the two (i.e. the innate desire to do good to fellow human beings). By the end of her time with us, while she acknowledged that what was being done was completely selfless, she recognized that spiritual warfare, deliverance and other such overtly spiritual activity was impossible to fully understand from a secular mindset. Her visit highlighted a few things in my mind, not the least of which was the fact that even the secular world recognizes the effectiveness of a powerful, city-transforming ministry. If New life Church had not had such a significant impact in the spiritual transformation of the city of Colorado Springs, it is doubtful that this reporter would have had any reason to come out and see for herself whether the stories she had heard were true. I recognize that it is arguable as to whether the transformations that have taken place over the years in Colorado Springs are as a direct result of the spiritual warfare (deliverance). However, if the premise upon which we base this assertion is the word of God, then we know that His word teaches in James chapter five that powerful prayer produces a tremendous harvest of positive change in the hearts and minds of people.

## The supernatural transformation of cities

The testimonies of the transformations of the cities of Cali, Kiambu, Hemet and Almolonga are well documented in the video "Transformations" produced by George Otis Jr. For the benefit of those readers who have not seen the video, let me share a little bit of the miraculous power of deliverance and spiritual warfare in altering the spiritual DNA of an entire community.

Cali, Colombia was once recognized as the drug capital of the world. The Cali Cartel was said to be the most organized and powerful organized crime group in history. Drug-related deaths were rampant throughout the city. Crime bosses controlled the law enforcement agencies through bribery and intimidation.

As the Church slowly but surely began to recognize their role in thwarting the advancement of these drug cartels, they began intense and organized praying and fasting. They studied the spiritual roots of the city using zoned maps of the city prepared by the government. They identified the ruling spirits over different areas of the city and began to break the strongholds of the occult, mediums and spirit guides that were so prevalent throughout the highest levels of civil and religious leadership. In 1995, they held their first major Christian rally in Cali, packing out a stadium with more than 50,000 people. The weekend of the rally the local newspapers reported that for the first time in a 48-hour period there were no homicides to report. Ten days later the first of seven leading drug barons was apprehended and taken into custody.

As the Christians continued to gain spiritual ground in the battle for their city, they used local football stadiums to host all night prayer vigils that would often boast more than 60,000 people in attendance. Sometimes as many as 15,000 people would be turned away because the stadium was jammed to capacity. The city officials of Cali quickly recognized that definite transformation was beginning to take place in their city with all the prayers and demonic warfare being waged by the Christians. They jumped on board and paid for the advertising, sound support and security for the prayer events in addition to providing free use of the 22,000-seat velodrome. The result was mass repentance, reconciliation, sustained prayer and the ultimate demise of the most powerful drug cartels in the world.

Kiambu, Kenya was rife with witchcraft, fortunetellers and the like. One particularly troublesome lady named "Mama Jane" set up such opposition against the Church by putting all sorts of little fetishes around their prayer meetings. The Church rose up in prayer against this demonic influx and "prayed Mama Jane out of town." After she moved out of Kiambu all the local bars closed, the churches began to grow and the crime rate dropped to one of the lowest in the country. As a result of this dramatic transformation people are moving in droves into Kiambu. The population has increased by 30%. Daily, over 400 intercessors gather to pray and do spiritual battle against the demonic forces that seek to regain control of the city of Kiambu.

California. In their effort to rid their city of the effects of these destructive influences, the Christians there employed spiritual mapping to demarcate their city and to pray together with specific direction. Within a short time, the most notorious gang in San Jacinto, known as the First Street Gang, had its entire membership accept the lordship of Jesus Christ. Since the advent of the united prayer efforts against the ruling territorial spirits in the area, church attendance has doubled in the past 10 years, rising to 14%. It is estimated that more than 40% of the entire police force and the local schoolteachers are born-again Christians. The city of Hemet has been completely transformed by the prayers and spiritual warfare against demonic forces that previously held the city in darkness.

Finally, the story of Almolonga, Guatemala is without parallel in the annals of recent Church history. Today, eight out of every ten residents is a born-again Christian, and people are fasting three or four days out of every week and holding all night prayer vigils every weekend. There are no jails in the city; they have all been converted for other uses due to the lack of crime.

It wasn't always like this though. The city used to be controlled by witchcraft, alcoholism, and violence. With the introduction of prayer and mass deliverance services, their churches began to grow again. They went from having 36 bars to just 3, and in 1994 the last of their four jails was closed. The growth of the city's agricultural base has paralleled its spiritual growth. What was once an arid valley has come to be known affectionately as "America's vegetable garden." The farmers make 40 deliveries a week on their Mercedes trucks—which they paid for in cash. They have three crop harvests a month and produce some of the largest vegetables grown anywhere.[3]

These are proven, documented testimonies of the transforming power of prayer, spiritual warfare and deliverance. They are not just stories that are designed to encourage us and make us feel good about being Christians. No! Resoundingly, no! These are more than stories. They are the evidence of God's heart for the nations of the world. These portraits of transformation are not just for Cali, Kiambu, Hemet and Almolonga, but are God's masterpieces that prove that His desire is to see the nations transformed and conformed into the image of Christ for all of time.

## Cities under siege

> "Now as He drew near, He saw the city and wept over it."
>
> - Luke 19: 41

After all is said and done, the most significant key to the successful transformation of our cities is possessing a deep, abiding passion for the city and its inhabitants. Amazingly, there are only a few recorded incidents of Jesus weeping in the scriptures. Each incident was motivated by a compassion for the lost and dying.

It cannot be overemphasized that the battle for the spiritual survival of our cities must be waged on a spiritual level. In Acts 17: 16, the Bible records, "Now while Paul waited for them at Athens, his spirit was provoked within him when he saw that the city was given over to idols." It is noteworthy that the entire city is referenced here and not just certain individuals, even though we know that there must have been those in the city that worshipped the one true God.

Clearly, then, the spiritual battle for our cities goes a long way in determining how much transformation they experience in the physical. If, as we previously read, adverse spiritual forces can control a city, then the transformation of that city is dependent on the influx of the truth of the gospel. In explaining this further, Paul exhorts that we flee from idolatry (I Corinthians 10: 14), which he identifies as a demonic manifestation. This is the only time the word idolatry is used in this context in the New Testament. It is the Greek word *kateidolos*,[2] which literally means opposition of a heathen god. This strengthens the notion that the proliferation of idolatry in a city is evidence of the control of demonic forces over that city.

It is only in the realization that our cities are given over to demonic entrenchment that we can adequately arm ourselves to fight the battle against the enemy. As in the case of the four cities mentioned previously, only a spiritual eye-opening can help us see the level of warfare that is arrayed against the Church from one city to the next. We would do well to recognize that the opposition of heathen gods is not found only in stone or brass idols, but is also manifest in the subtleties of many of our cultural norms.

It is imperative that the Church is uncompromising in her moral stand against the dictates of our culture that are in direct opposition to the mandates of scripture. As long as we allow our cities to be overrun by moral and spiritual perversion along with all the attendant trappings of a post-Christian society, we run the very real danger of losing the battle for spiritual control of our cities and, subsequently, their complete and total transformation.

# Maintaining Your Deliverance and Walking in Freedom

I recently heard of an experiment involving baby elephants. Soon after an elephant is born it is chained around the ankle to a stake driven in the ground. After several failed attempts, the elephant learns that it can't walk beyond the length of the chain. As the elephant grows, the size of the chain around its ankle is simply increased. When fully grown, an elephant easily weighs 2 tons or more and is fully capable of ripping out the chain. Fascinatingly, though, the elephant no longer even tries. It has been programmed to believe that the length of the chain is the extent of its freedom to move.

A similar experiment is done using barracuda sharks. One shark is placed in a tank and fed mackerel for a while. After some time, a clear piece of glass is inserted into the tank, dividing it into two sections. The barracuda is placed in one section; lots of mackerel is dumped in the other. Every time the barracuda attempts to attack the mackerel it bumps up against the glass. After numerous failed attempts it gives up. Then, when the piece of glass is removed, the shark doesn't bother trying for the mackerel at all.

Freedom can be a deceptive thing for elephants, barracuda sharks…and especially for humans. Consider the mindset of the elephant having been chained to the stake all of its life. It is unable to even entertain the thought that there is freedom available at the mere lifting of its massive foot. Likewise, the devil has programmed many Christians to believe that they are chained to the bondage of their "addictions" forever. Even after the heavy price for redemption paid by Christ on the cross of Calvary, they still believe that there is no way out. Still others act as if their freedom in Christ is a license to sin willfully and then ask for forgiveness, forgetting that there are spiritual consequences to sin.

Not long ago, I read the biography *Narrative of the Life of Frederick Douglass*. Having been born into a life of slavery, Frederick Douglass secretly taught himself to read and write, even though it was a crime punishable by death. In his introduction to the book, Peter J Gomes writes, "Douglass did not know the date of his own birth, an ignorance he regarded as one of the worst legacies of his bondage, but he assumed that he had been born in 1817, perhaps in February, to a white man, perhaps his master, and a slave woman whom he hardly knew and who died before he was seven years old…no individual identity was meant to survive in a system where slaves were regarded as real estate…During the course of his escape to the North, he became first Frederick Stanley, and then Frederick Johnson, the name of abolitionist benefactors in New Bedford, Massachusetts. There were however, so many Johnsons in that city of refuge that he was obliged to change his name again. The benefactor Johnson was in the midst of reading Sir Walter Scott's novel *The Lady of the Lake*, and in response to young Frederick's need of a new name gave him the Scottish surname by which he would be forever known, Frederick *Douglass*…[1] 'As a child,' writes W. E. B. DuBois of Douglass, 'he experienced neglect and cruelty, indulgence and hard work; but particularly the tyranny and circumscription of an ambitious human being who was legally classed as real estate.' Ambition, sensitivity, and a high degree of self-consciousness created in the young slave Douglass an unquenchable thirst for freedom, and he became what every slave master feared, a smart and uppity Negro ***who would be content with nothing less than his freedom***."[2]

Frederick Douglass dates his freedom from September 3, 1838. He became Secretary of the Santo Domingo Commission, Recorder of Deeds in the District of Columbia, and United States Minister to Haiti. He died in 1895 a free man.

It really doesn't matter what your heritage is. You may come from a long ancestral line of alcoholics and underachievers. It may be that your lineage boasts of nothing but failed marriages and sexual indiscretions, or it could be that you suffered intense emotional and physical abuse as a child. Whatever your family legacy, like Frederick Douglass, you can develop such an insatiable desire for freedom that you are unwilling to settle for anything less. Your relationship with Jesus gives you the right to a new name and a new heritage. No longer do the sins of your ancestral heritage or the poor choices of the past have a right to a hold over your future. You have the right to live and die a free man.

As stated earlier, there is no worse bondage than bondage to sin. If sin is walking outside of the will of God (missing the mark), then continued acceptance of a spiritual state of bondage that habitually causes us to walk outside of the will of God is most definitely sin. The memoirs of slaves like Douglass and DuBois teach us that only one who has been enslaved and then experienced what it's like to walk in true freedom can have a true appreciation for freedom. As Christians who were held captive by the deceptions of Satan for so long before experiencing the freedom that Christ purchased for us on the cross, we must walk out our Christian experience as people who understand and appreciate the true value of freedom from sin and demonic bondage.

## Experiencing freedom

In her own words, this is the personal testimony of Julia, a woman who went from bondage to the occult to freedom in Christ:

> "I have entitled this "Julia's Testimony," but in reality this is an example of God's doing, His experience, through my empty eyes. I lived in my own black hole created through fear, confusion through depression, and an agonizing pain of living

each day not knowing who or what I was. I was tormented daily for fourteen years of my life by the ongoing process of my possession by spirits who I thought were just some part of me that I couldn't understand. That in itself was the basis of my confusion; the fact that I didn't understand made me believe even more that I was crazy and I had deluded myself into a secluded part of my mind where the real me sat and cried alone. I had had many unfortunate experiences with demons that should have awakened me and made me realize that it wasn't me. The following are only a few of many that I will share. They are the only ones, for now, that I am able to speak of with you and a few others who know my situation.

I would lie in bed awake, unable to sleep, bewildered by the haunting thoughts running through my head. These thoughts would come at me very fast and all at once that I would sit and stare into nothing, as if I was in a hypnotic trance that I could do nothing about. The thoughts would consist of me dying numerous deaths, thoughts of the world that angered and saddened me, thoughts of my twin sister, and thoughts of the past that was still very much with me. Then I would come to, to the point where I could blink again, but now it was physically impossible for me to move. I was, for these moments, paralyzed from the neck down.

Something heavy would surround me and eventually would be right on top of me and my eyes would begin to grown heavy to the point where I struggled to keep them open. I would then feel something strange but very real going through me at one side of my uterus. This would last for what seemed like forever at first. Then, when it began to happen at least once a week, it became more of a weekly routine that I was expecting and unknowingly, began to crave. Ultimately, I became addicted to it.

Going back now, after this strange sensation of something going through my uterus, I would begin to feel my head jerk to the side, usually the side towards where this was going on in my stomach. It would jerk so hard that it would hurt. The only thing stopping it from jerking even more towards my back was my pillow and bed. During these happenings, I would hear and see things. Once I saw the figure of a man, basically just a sort of dark shadowy figure but very tall. He might have been as tall as the ceiling as I remember. This man was calling my name, just repeating it and each time his voice would get closer and I seemed to be getting weaker. Finally, after struggling with every breath and strength in me, I broke free. Another time, I fell into this trance, but this time I first began to hear a dog bark, and then I saw things. I saw an image of my profile with red all around me, then I heard the radio—which was off—turn on and change stations to things I could not identify. I then heard a buzzing, sort of chanting sound coming from all around me. I saw little black images just surrounding me until I finally broke free again.

These experiences were something that became a part of my lifestyle. It happened so often that I became used to it and sort of comfortable with it. It was something I learned not to fear, just accept. Falling asleep to it was my solution. It would happen, I would let it and then I would fall asleep, sometimes in the middle of the process. I would wake up with scars on my body to remind me of what I belonged to and what I had been unfortunately drawn to.

Don't misunderstand me, this wasn't something that I had agreed to, or if I had a choice, would have chosen. This was something that I later found out was a curse, something that my father had bestowed upon me through his actions and words towards me and my sisters and brother. Fortunately, I was the only one to have gone through this and for that I thank God. I have forgiven my father because I know it wasn't him and it still isn't him that rejects me.

This possession that I dealt with became very strong; so strong to the point where suicidal attempts were not a challenge, just a past time that was combined with alcohol. My attempts included trying to jump off of a bridge, choking myself to the point where I would faint, trying to stab myself a few times, etc. God really has become real to me just thinking about all of this these past few weeks. Without Him I could not have physically survived the things I went through. He always came through by having the right person or people there at the times of these attempts. I also believe that some of the witnesses to this have come to the Lord just by seeing these things happen to me. They could not explain it and the idea that alcohol could do this to me was impossible to believe, although it was probably easier for some to believe than a demonic influence.

The events during which I tried to choke myself were quite a different experience, however. They occurred just a few times but they had the greatest impact on me. It would be a couple of hours after I would have had a couple, or should I say a lot, of shots of an alcoholic beverage. I would pass out, then awake with sudden uncontrollable strength and it was almost as if I wasn't even there anymore. I would cling tightly to a certain necklace that I had bought in Puerto Vallarta one summer. It somehow calmed me with thoughts of dying. Then out of nowhere, I would reach towards my neck with more strength than I could ever imagine having, and begin choking myself. The people around me, which included several guys and girls, tried pulling my hands away. At this time, I would be gagging for my life to the point where I would literally pass out right before they were able to pull my hands away.

I would rest for a while after this and at these times more than ever, I could feel the presence of the spirits. It was so strong and right there in front of me. My ears became very sensitive and I could hear them chanting and laughing in echoed voices. I also heard crying, which confused me. I would fall asleep listening to this.

These experiences, again, are only a few but they show and give an idea of where I came from. I was led to Colorado for the second time this past October, where I met with Pastor Joseph for the second time. Our first encounter was under the circumstances of one of my "episodes," at a TAG [high school] service. The song "Consuming Fire" had begun to play, and I was "gone." I felt claustrophobic and scared. Everything and everyone seemed fuzzy and unreal. I was saying things to try and calm myself, but I couldn't. Then I felt this fear, this rapid fear, all around and I shot a look towards the back. There was Pastor Joseph with my cousin Debbie [not her real name]. Immediately, I looked for a way out. I understand now that this was not me, only myself looking through the eyes of this thing, unable to react. Pastor Joseph came towards me and I began to cling to my hair and face, not being able to do anything but wait. As he approached, I jumped back to the chair behind me and just stared at him with a deep evil set look. Eventually he, accompanied by two others, led me to a room upstairs where they tried to communicate with me, not the spirits. It was impossible. I ran out and waited for Debbie to come back down. We left with the promise that I would see him that following week. I went but, sadly, accomplished nothing.

A couple of months later, I returned to California, but this time I was going to be faced with more than I could have imagined. That year went by with many struggles and eventually I was drawn back to Colorado, when I got accepted to an art school in Denver. About a week before I was to begin, something came up and my enrolment was canceled. Angered by the whole situation, I chose to leave home again and live with another cousin in Colorado Springs. This was in October.

I didn't go in to see Pastor Joseph until I returned from my vacation in California shortly after Christmas, somewhere at the end of January. I had had a frightening experience that I needed answers to. I set up a meeting and so it began, the first step to my realization and acceptance of God. The first couple of meetings, I struggled through, my body shaking uncontrollably every time I sat next to Pastor Joseph. Finally, it came time for a deliverance session, which I reluctantly went to, but I knew it had to be done. It was quite an experience, which lasted a few hours. I was not completely set free, but there was a difference and I knew that the rest was up to me.

The next two weeks, I was faced with an enormous amount of depression and a craving for the spirits to come back, for me to feel their presence. I sometimes lay in my bed, just waiting, waiting for any little sign that they were still there with me. Then it would hit me. The idea of me wanting the experience was unbearable and I would get up and try to talk to God. Eventually I worked through it and two weeks ago, I asked God, the Lord Jesus Christ and my Savior, into my heart where I plan to keep Him always, first and foremost. At first, I was not too excited, but now after slowly seeing and feeling the difference, I am forever grateful. Grateful to God for never giving up on me, even after I slammed the door shut numerous times. He kept knocking and each time, He knocked harder. I am also grateful to those who cared enough to pray for me.

> I now know what it is to live in order to live and not live to die. I now have this overwhelming sense of ***freedom***, joy and passion to be one of God's servants and children. I do not pray anymore for the will to live; I pray that God may use me and that in everything I do, I may please Him to the point where He can be proud of who I have become in Christ."

Julia's testimony is proof that we, all too often, become captives to the limitations that Satan attempts to place around us. The bondage of spiritual darkness is seemingly a never-ending web drawing tighter and tighter around us. Fortunately, her testimony also attests to the fact that when we seek deliverance and freedom from the snares of the devil, God has made adequate provision for us to receive that freedom.

## God's provision for freedom

There are three widely accepted aspects of walking in and maintaining your deliverance (aspects that I personally subscribe to). They are prayer, studying the Word of God, and confessing the Scriptures (praying the Scriptures specifically). These are obviously not all-inclusive, but certainly provide an adequate enough understanding for a Christian to continually walk in freedom from demonic bondage.

## Prayer

The book of James declares "...the effective, fervent prayer of a righteous man makes tremendous power available" (James 5: 16). Throughout the scriptures, we are reminded of the efficacy of prayer and its ability to bring comfort in times of sorrow, and deliverance in times of desperate need. Jesus Himself prayed so fervently in the Garden of Gethsemane that the Bible says that his perspiration came down as drops of blood. As He prayed, His disciples slept. He challenged them, saying, "Watch and pray so that you will not fall into temptation. The spirit is willing, but the flesh is weak."(Mark 14: 38)

We know how the story ends. His disciples, weakened by their inability to stay awake and pray, are scattered in every direction the moment temptation arrives in form of Judas Iscariot and the Roman centurions.

But prayer is not complicated. It is not reserved for the "called," neither is it reserved only for occasions where divine intervention is obviously needed. Prayer is communing with the heart of God. It is reminding God of His promises to you. It is enjoying His undivided attention as you meet with Him in the "secret place."

If prayer is communicating with God, then it is also a way to guarantee that we are walking in the will of God. It is extremely unlikely that one who is in constant communion with God would at the same time be living a willfully disobedient and carnal life. One of my favorite sayings is, "If you're outside and you don't want to get wet from the rain, then carry an umbrella." Not in the least bit profound, I admit. But consider this: If the world system in which we live is controlled by the devil (Satan is the god of this world - II Corinthians 4: 4) and we liken his demonic attacks on Christians to the rain, then the umbrella that shields us from the rain is our intimacy with God through prayer and the knowledge of His unfailing love towards us (see Isaiah 59: 19).

## Study to show yourself approved

Paul, in writing to Timothy, exhorts him with the following words:

> "Study to show thyself approved unto God, a workman that needeth not to be ashamed, rightly dividing the word of truth .
> - 2 Timothy 2:15, KJV

Study is the only way to acquire knowledge. In order for us to be effective witnesses for Christ, we must have intimate knowledge of him.

Paul, recognizing this, counsels Timothy to make it a focal point for the effectiveness of his ministry.

Likewise, in Mark 3: 3, Jesus called to the mountaintop all those that He wanted and they came to Him. Verse 4 emphasizes that the primary reason for the call was that they might be with him. Second, he wanted them to become effective witnesses, cast out demons and heal the sick. But all of these secondary reasons were predicated on the first being fulfilled—"That they might be with Him." Being with Him and being His disciples required a commitment of their time and resources in order to study His life and learn His purpose for their lives.

There is continuous counsel in the Scriptures that encourages the Christian to give himself diligently to the study of God's Word. Imagine that you purchased a new bicycle that you had seen displayed on the shop floor. You pay for the bike and drive around to the merchandise pick-up window. You hand the attendant your ticket, expecting to get the bike all ready to go. The attendant hands you a box that contains a gazillion parts and the manufacturer's assembly instructions. If you ever hope to assemble that bike so that it functions as the manufacturer intended, you must spend the first few moments (or hours!) studying and dissecting the instructions. The same principle applies to understanding and walking in God's perfect will for our lives. The Bible is required reading to identify all that God has determined for us in order that we may function according to our Maker's "specifications."

There are no shortcuts to becoming an effective and overcoming Christian. Studying the Word of God is a prerequisite to understanding Him and His purpose. The more you study about Him, the more you realize how much there is to know about Him. To paraphrase a popular saying, to know Him is to love Him.

## Thy word is a light unto my path

Confessing the scriptures can be likened to a cow, chewing cud. The cow grazes endlessly for hours and then finds a secluded spot where it settles down and begins to regurgitate all the grass it has consumed. It masticates the grass extracting all the nutrients until it is satisfied and then it spits out the unneeded dregs.

In much the same way, the Christian studies the word of God diligently; storing it away in his spirit until a circumstance arises that requires the application of a particular scripture. Like the cow, chewing cud, the Christian regurgitates the word and continues to speak or confess it over his situation. Faith begins to rise as the word is confessed (this can be likened to the cow drawing the nutrients out of the grass it has eaten). If, as the scripture says, faith comes by hearing the word of God (Romans 10: 17), then the continued confession of the scriptures over situations and circumstances that mitigate against us will ultimately bring faith and consequently victory. The bible teaches that without faith it is impossible to please God (Hebrews 11: 6). Clearly then, with faith being a prerequisite for pleasing God, the Christian seeking to continually walk in freedom from demonic bondage must continually stay in the place of confessing the word of God over his or her circumstances.

The much maligned saying, "confession brings possession" was never truer than under these circumstances. To "possess" all that God has determined for us requires us to believe that He exists and that He rewards those who earnestly seek Him (Hebrews 11: 6 NIV). If we believe that, then we are more likely to exercise our faith by confessing the scriptures over different areas of our lives daily so that our "spiritual muscles" are flexed and strengthened in those areas continually.

## Free at Last

On August 28, 1963 the words of Martin Luther King, Jr. were immortalized forever in his famous, "I Have a Dream" speech. Though these words were delivered as a cry against the tyranny of racial inequality and injustice, they ring just as true today as a rejection of the tyranny and bondage of spiritual slavery:

> And when this happens, and when we allow ***freedom*** to ring, when we let it ring from every village and every hamlet, from every state and every city, we will be able to speed up that day when all of God's children, black men and white men, Jews and Gentiles, Protestants and Catholics, will be able to join

> hands and sing in the words of that old Negro spiritual, ***'Free at last! Free at last! Thank God Almighty, we are free at last!'"*** [3]

What an incredible hour that will be for the Church, when we are walking in such a revelation of the freedom that was purchased for us on the cross. What an hour that will be when the world sees the Church in all of her resplendent glory and desires to possess the things that we possess: true freedom in Christ.

I would do you a disservice however, if I left you thinking that freedom in Christ is a one-step event as opposed to a continuing process. Because we live in a world that is so tainted by sin, the need for continued self-deliverance cannot be overemphasized. I can best illustrate this point with the following short story:

> When Pablo Casals reached 95, a young reporter threw him a question: "Mr. Casals, you are 95 and the greatest cellist that ever lived. Why do you still practice six hours a day?" Mr. Casals answered, "Because I think I'm making progress." [4]

Why do we continue to seek freedom and deliverance? Why do we strive to better ourselves and strengthen our relationships with God and others? Because we know we are making progress.

# Footnotes

Chapter 1
James Strong, *The New Strong's Exhaustive Concordance of The Bible,* (Thomas Nelson Publishers, Nashville, 1984)
Ibid. p. 72 (Greek)
Ibid. p. 78 (Greek)
Ibid. p. 16 (Greek)
Ibid. p. 8 (Greek)
Ibid. p. 44 (Greek)
Ibid. p. 44 (Greek)

Chapter 2
James Strong, *The New Strong's Exhaustive Concordance of The Bible,* (Thomas Nelson Publishers, Nashville, 1984)

Chapter 3
James Strong, *The New Strong's Exhaustive Concordance of The Bible,* (Thomas Nelson Publishers, Nashville, 1984)
Lester Sumrall, *Dispensations,* (LeSea Publishing, South Bend, 1987)

Chapter 4
Max Lucado, *He Chose the Nails,* (Word Publishing, Nashville, 2000)

Chapter 5
James Strong, *The New Strong's Exhaustive Concordance of The Bible,* (Thomas Nelson Publishers, Nashville, 1984)
Flavius Josephus, *The Antiquities of The Jews,* (Hendrickson Publishers, Peabody, 1987)
Lester Sumrall, *The Gifts and Ministries of The Holy Spirit,* (LeSea Publishing, South Bend, 1990)
Kenneth E. Hagin, *The Holy Spirit and His Gifts,* (Harrison House, Tulsa, 1995)
Strong, *Concordance,* p. 47
W. E. Vine, Merrill F. Unger, William White, Jr., *Vine's Complete Expository Dictionary of Old and New Testament Words,* (Thomas Nelson Publishers, Nashville 1984)
Marcus Tanner, *U.K. News Website,* (October 30, 1998)
Ted Haggard, *Charisma Magazine,* (Strang Communications, Lake Mary, 1998)
Vernon J. McGee, *Joshua and Judges,* (Griffin Printing and Lithograph Coy, Inc., Glendale, 1976)

Chapter 6
Chuck Colson, *Breakpoint with Chuck Colson,* (Prison Fellowship Ministries, Washington D.C., 1999)
Richard G. Tansey, Fred S. Kleiner, *Gardner's Art Through The Ages,* (Harcourt Brace College Publishers, Fort Worth, 1996)
Ibid. pp. 66 – 97

Chapter 9
David L. Brown, *The Dark Side of Halloween,* (Logosresourcepages.org, 1990)
*The History of Halloween,* (Historychannel.com, 2001)
C. Peter Wagner, *Churchquake,* (Regal Books, Ventura, 1999)
George Otis Jr., *Transformations,* (The Sentinel Group, Lynnwood, 1999)

Chapter 10
Frederick Douglass, *Narrative of The Life of Frederick Douglass,* (Signet Classic, New York, 1997)
W. E. B. Du Bois, *The Souls of Black Folk,* (Signet Classic, New York, 1995)
Coretta Scott King, *The Words of Martin Luther King, Jr.* (Newmarket Press, New York, 1983)
*Growth,* (Sermonillustrations.com, 2000)